What people

The Shapi

Richard Harries' autobiography is a deeply moving account of an extraordinary life of our times. It challenges the faithless and humbles the indolent.

Sir Simon Jenkins

If you know Richard Harries, it's probably through listening to "Thought for the Day" on the *Today* programme on BBC Radio 4. This is the story behind the voice. And it's gripping – human, humane, often humorous, frequently moving, it's an account of the unexpected life of a remarkable man – a soldier turned priest, a bishop and a broadcaster, a husband and a father, whose private life has known profound challenges and whose public life has known all sorts of controversy. With a fascinating cast list – that includes the Queen, prelates and prime ministers – this is a compelling autobiography that is as life-enhancing as it is revealing, because through it runs the golden thread of Richard Harries' faith.

Gyles Brandreth

Richard Harries is one of the towering figures of the Church of England in the past fifty years. In this wise, charming and challenging account of a lifetime's service of the Church and the gospel, he observes that "the first task of a Diocesan Bishop is to appoint good people, and the second is to let them get on with it." As one of those appointed by him, and then given space to grow and flourish – and make mistakes and be picked up – I am grateful for this book. It will help many Christian leaders reflect on their own formation and journey and the exercise of ministry. For Richard this ministry was always focussed on the

world Christ came to save. His vision is expansive, generous and intellectually stimulating. And of course, it is beautifully written in simple, pithy elegant prose. Reading it will save some leaders today from focussing too much on themselves and on the institution of the Church. Full of wit and wisdom, it will lift your sights.
Stephen Cottrell, Archbishop of York

I loved *The Shaping of a Soul* by Richard Harries. It is searingly honest, full of intellectual and spiritual challenge, and surprisingly amusing about aspects of his life. He covers spiritual, religious, political, moral, ethical and human issues – often combined – and he makes us think about why faith matters, and indeed how it can be built up again in the modern, western world.
Julia Neuberger, Rabbi and member of the House of Lords

As a non-believer I spent 33 years on *Today* trying (and failing) to persuade the BBC to drop "Thought for the Day". They refused. Richard Harries is a shining example of why they just *might* have been right. If there's one justification for "Thought" it's that it should make the listener think. That's what Richard did. Without fail. This absorbing book of his spiritual journey and engagement with the great issues of our time does the same. It proves that he's the greatest Archbishop of Canterbury the Anglican Church never had.
John Humphrys

And about Richard Harries
In Richard, the twentieth-century Church of England – and the twenty-first-century Church of England for the matter – has had one of its truly great and memorable figures. He is one of our greatest Christian intellectuals.
Rowan Williams, former Archbishop of Canterbury

While I am agnostic about the existence of God, I am not agnostic about life after death. I am sure that belief in it is an illusion. However, if – which God forbid – I should undergo a death bed conversion, there is no Christian priest I would rather have at my bedside than Richard Harries.

Sir Antony Kenny, philosopher and former Master of Baliol

The Shaping of a Soul

A life taken by Surprise

The Shaping of a Soul

A life taken by Surprise

Richard Harries

CHRISTIAN ALTERNATIVE
BOOKS

Winchester, UK
Washington, USA

JOHN HUNT PUBLISHING

First published by Christian Alternative Books, 2024
Christian Alternative Books is an imprint of John Hunt Publishing Ltd.,
No. 3 East St., Alresford, Hampshire SO24 9EE, UK
office@jhpbooks.com
www.johnhuntpublishing.com
www.christian-alternative.com

For distributor details and how to order please visit the 'Ordering' section on our website.

ISBN: 978 1 80341 162 0
978 1 80341 163 7 (ebook)
Library of Congress Control Number: 2022930304

A CIP catalogue record for this book is available from the British Library.

Design: Lapiz Digital Services

UK: Printed and bound by CPI Group (UK) Ltd, Croydon, CR0 4YY
US: Printed and bound by Thomson-Shore, 7300 West Joy Road, Dexter, MI 48130

We operate a distinctive and ethical publishing philosophy in
all areas of our business, from our global network of authors to
production and worldwide distribution.

Contents

For Jo, Mark and Cilla, Clare and Sylvain, Luke, Toby, Ben and Sophie with much love

Richard Harries was serving as a soldier in Germany when he suddenly had an overwhelming sense that God was calling him to be ordained. He had virtually no religious background but, like Martin Luther, he could do no other. This is the story of a man who has engaged in some of the major issues of our time and who for fifty years has been a much loved voice on "Thought for the Day" in the *Today* programme. Bishop of Oxford from 1987 to 2006, he was made a Life Peer on his retirement and remains active in the House of Lords as Lord Harries of Pentregarth. In a life repeatedly taken by surprise, he tells how he is still able to retain his faith even in our present highly secular and sceptical society.

Richard Harries is the author of more than thirty books. These include

God outside the box: why spiritual people object to Christianity
(0-281-05522-X)

The beauty and the horror: searching for God in a suffering world
(978-0-281-07695-6)

After the evil: Christianity and Judaism in the shadow of the holocaust (0-19-926313-2)

The Image of Christ in modern art (97814094633825)

Haunted by Christ: modern writers and the struggle for faith
(978-0-281-07934-6)

Seeing God in art: the Christian faith in 30 images
(978-0-281-08382-4)

Hearing God in poetry: fifty poems for Lent and Easter
(978-0-281-08629-0)

The Re-enchantment of morality: wisdom for a troubled world
(978-0-281-05947-8) which was shortlisted for the
Michael Ramsey prize.

Art and the beauty of God (0-264-67510-X) which was selected as a book of the year by Anthony Burgess in *The Observer*

Preface

In 1958 I was serving as a Lieutenant in the Royal Corps of Signals in the British Army of the Rhine. I was looking forward to going up to Cambridge, at the army's expense, to do a degree in Mechanical Engineering, having managed to pass Part I of the Tripos, which in those days you had to take in addition to the equivalent of what are now A-levels. It was a good time, with plenty of sport, and much to look forward to.

By some mysterious process a few months before a thought had come into my mind: "Wouldn't it be funny if one day you were ordained." From time to time, it slipped quietly into my mind again and as quickly disappeared. Then another equally mysterious thought came, "Wouldn't it be nice when I retire from the army as a General with a good pension to spend my life as a country parson." Then, smack, bang, the words formed in my mind. "Well, if that's what you are meant to be doing, you had better do it now." An inner volcano exploded. Like Martin Luther I could do no other.

It was very strange. No clergyman had ever been a role model. In fact, just the opposite. The chaplain at my prep school struck me as a weed. The chaplain at Wellington College, where I was at school was genial but I did not know him and he did not spiritually attract me. There were no clergy in my family. Moreover, I had no experience of ordinary church life as a member of a congregation. My family had not gone to Church when I was young. I can indeed remember the one solitary time we did go when I was a teenager. The Vicar of the neighbouring village of Stoke d'Abernon had a reputation as a good preacher, so my parents decided to go one Sunday to hear him and took me with them. I found the sermon an unbearable piece of ham acting. So there was absolutely nothing about the clergy or church life to attract me, and I had no experience at all of parish life. I certainly wouldn't even be put forward for a selection conference these days.

That dramatic inner explosion, coming out of the blue, has been the most formative experience of my life. The only other that compares with it is falling in love with the girl who is my wife and proposing to her four days later. That was the beginning of a life taken by surprise.

This is not a straightforward biography. As my title, *The Shaping of a Soul*, indicates, I want to understand the main influences on my life and explore why I believe what I believe and why, so far as anyone can know, why I am who I am. As mentioned, I came from a background in which religion played no significant place to find myself out of the blue taken hold of by what I believed was the call of God. I want to trace a path through the experiences of my life and its intellectual challenges to where I am now, still a person of faith but living in a cultural milieu which is highly secular and dominated by those whom Schleiermacher in the nineteenth century described as the "cultured despisers" of religion. How does my faith stand now in such a different intellectual environment? Why am I still gripped by the Christian faith when so many decent people are either indifferent or highly sceptical?

I use the word soul in a Hebrew sense to indicate the whole person. I do not just mean what the philosopher Gilbert Ryle termed a box within a box within a box. However, I do believe that everyone has a spiritual orientation and destiny and that is why I use the word soul. As this is a book which seeks to express gratitude to those who have influenced me for good by their life or writings, it is also a work of *pietas*. The older I get the more conscious I am that I have met so many wonderful people. The American intellectual Susan Sontag once described herself as a great admirer. So am I, and in a world beset by cynicism I am happy to be someone who tries to appreciate people and the world around me. I claim no credit for this, of course. It must be due to the way I was brought up. Especially I would like to express my gratitude for those whose prayers and kindness have helped shape me, wonderful friends, not least those who have sadly died, and above all my wife, Jo, and family to whom the book is dedicated.

Theologians may puzzle their heads about dogmas as they will, the religion of gratitude cannot mislead us. Of that we are sure, and gratitude is the handmaid to hope, and hope the harbinger of faith. I look abroad upon nature, I think of the best part of our species, I lean upon my friends, and I meditate upon the scriptures, especially the Gospel of St John, and my creed rises up of itself, with the ease of an exhalation, yet a fabric of adamant.
(William Wordsworth, Letter to Sir George Beaumont, 28 May 1825)

We bless thee for our creation, preservation, and all the blessings of this life; but above all, for thine inestimable love in the redemption of the world by our Lord Jesus Christ; for the means of grace and for the hope of glory.
(Prayer of General Thanksgiving, Book of Common Prayer)

The drawing of this love and the voice of this calling.
(*The Cloud of Unknowing,* quoted by T.S. Eliot in *Little Gidding*)

I tell my story for love of your love
(St Augustine, *Confessions*, Book XI (1))

I make my prayer through our Lord Jesus Christ your Son. By him you sought us when we were not seeking you. But you sought us that we should seek you.
(Book X)

Chapter 1

The matrix

1936–41

Freud said that he who is the favourite of his mother goes through life with the sense of a conqueror. I don't think I have ever had the sense of being a conqueror, nor did I think of myself as the favourite, but I obviously did know myself as deeply wanted. My mother, a warm, friendly person who liked babies, clearly bonded with me – and there is surely no greater gift a child can receive than to experience that bond from a parent or parental figure. She was a strong-willed person and as I and my sister, Linda, grew up our wills often came into conflict with hers and this was not perhaps the aspect of mothering she was best at handling. But as a baby, and as an infant too young to answer back, her warm physical mothering was what any baby needs more than anything else.

My mother's family lived at Rowberry in Donnington St Mary, Dorset, where her father, my grandfather, was the village doctor. One day he left his wife and went off with the Vicar's daughter, who was helping to look after the children to set up a new medical practice in another part of the country. He left a pregnant wife and 6 children. My grandmother refused to divorce him and his name was never mentioned. I never met him and I knew absolutely nothing about him until I was an adult. The 6 children, the last baby having died, all rallied round their mother and were solicitous of her welfare for the rest of her life, but it clearly left a deep scar in her and the whole family. She had been a good-looking women when young but I suspect became rather bitter. I remember an incident when she was looking after my sister and myself when my parents were abroad. We children happily played all day on the beach

5

obviously oblivious of the fact she might have some needs of her own, because one evening she exploded at supper and told us we were not considering her feelings at all. Some years after she died, I had a strange, disturbing experience of her soul, as it were, fluttering to keep alive before it disappeared and perished everlastingly. As I have changed my views on eternal salvation, I do not believe that dream reflected the truth.

One effect of my grandfather leaving was that there was never a great deal of money around. No doubt this was one reason why my mother was sent to school in a convent in Belgium. It was, I suspect, from the nuns, of whom she spoke fondly, that something of the faith got into her.

My mother was a very practical woman and did much of the painting and decoration herself, at least until she could persuade me to do it. This fitted in with her frugal nature, and as a child we never stayed in hotels or ate out at restaurants. She was notorious for making a single cigarette last a couple of days, taking a puff or two and then snipping it off and saving it. Her brothers and sisters, the Bathurst Browns, were decent people who enjoyed the simple pleasures of life like golf and beer.

On my father's side my grandfather was born and brought up at Glanmyddyfi, a small farm on the outskirts of Llandeilo, Carmarthenshire, where he later ran an ironmongers and early cycle shop. It was obviously successful for the family lived in the old vicarage, now an old people's home. Although Welsh was his first language, he brought up my father to speak English and make his way in an English speaking empire. I never heard my father speak Welsh. My grandfather retired to New Quay, Ceredigion, where his wife, my grandmother, came from, and they lived at 2, Pentregarth. She died before I really knew her but my grandfather was a vivid character who invented useful household devices in his workshop.

Because we moved around as a child, and because my parents were abroad for some years, New Quay was an element of continuity in my life. It was where I always went for holidays and why despite being thoroughly anglicised, I think of myself as Welsh. This also has something to do with the way Welsh people really seem to enjoy the company of children. In contrast to the English for whom the main requirement too often is that they conform and behave, the Welsh welcome children. Certainly I was always made to feel warmly welcome. This was no doubt helped by the fact that when you visited someone they gave you a little present, usually money or chocolate, and when you left at the end of the holidays, again there was another present of money. I write more fully about my Welsh roots in the next chapter.

My father made a very different life for himself compared with that in either Llandeilo or New Quay. After Sandhurst he was commissioned in the Welsh Regiment and then had the foresight to transfer to the Royal Corps of Signals when it was formed in the early 1920s. He was a man who liked everything in life structured and well ordered. I find myself the same. It shows in little things like wanting the bread sliced neatly and the dishwasher loaded with everything in its proper place. Fathers in those days were not hands-on parents, besides which he was away abroad for much of the time. Nor was ours a family which encouraged any real discussion on intimate matters, so I cannot say I was close to my father but certainly when I was making my way in life, from Sandhurst onwards, we got on well and he was always very supportive and interested in what I was doing. In mid-life, when he was on a tour of duty in the far East, he obviously went through some kind of crisis. He had been both overweight and a heavy smoker. He gave up cigarettes and went on diets. He also started being interested in religion, reading people like Ouspensky and Gurdjieff, and eventually going to church. But as my mother said, for the first twenty years she knew him she could not get him near a church even for Christmas day. Although holding a senior military rank he was a considerate man, known for his courtesy to everyone. When he retired as Commandant at Catterick with nine regiments under his command, he joined John Lewis as Superintendent of Personnel. But he had to begin by serving six months on the shop floor. It did not seem to bother him in the least.

I am grateful for the love of both my parents, especially for the physical warmth of my mother and for my father's steadfastness and courtesy. I have been blessed with a fine brother, Charles, an engineer with a skilled hand and eye who has pursued his artistic work despite having MS and Linda who has brought up a flourishing family and is a very supportive sister. I wish our home had been one with more culture, especially music, in it. It would also have been enriched by more conversation about things which matter, and a more questioning approach to life. But I did receive the most essential gift of all which was the stability provided by the love and support of my parents. Because they were abroad a lot and I was sent away to school, their absence left its mark but this did not take away from the early firm foundation or the later strong support.

My parents, Bill and Greta.

Chapter 2

Stars and stripes

1941–4

When war broke out my mother, sister, Linda, and I moved down to New Quay, to what my mother called her funk hole. As my father was then stationed at Woolwich, an obvious target for bombs, and we lived nearby at Eltham, it made sense. My father was then posted to France but was switched at the last moment to go to Washington to liaise between the Royal Signals, and the US signal corps especially in relation to the purchase and use of signal equipment. The rest of the family followed sailing from Liverpool on 25 August 1941 on SS Modessa, a commandeered orange cargo boat. We went by taxi from New Quay. I was terribly car sick but very impressed by the long tunnel under the Mersey. It was a time when ships were being sunk every week in mid Atlantic by German U boats, with thousands of lives lost. To avoid this, we sailed as part of a large convoy via Iceland and Greenland, taking more than three weeks, not arriving until 17 September. I gather we kept our life jackets on all the time.

In Washington we lived at 2843 Chesapeake Street, an attractive white shutter board house with our spacious tan Buick parked outside. I went to the large local school, where we were reminded one day by the presence of a tank parked on the playground that there was a war on. Chocolate milk was available in the break but my mother thought that ordinary milk was good enough. But it was a happy time, and the warmth and generosity of the American people meant that I have never shared the knee jerk anti-Americanism that has characterised so much European thought in recent years. I remember especially the vivid colours at Christmas time, bright red with sparkling lights; the sounds of cicadas in the evening at the British

Embassy, and the chatter of a cocktail party at home after we children had gone to bed. We lived opposite a large American High School, and we could see pupils "Canoodling", as my mother called it, in the bushes. Many of them arrived at school by car. It all seemed rather advanced by British standards.

I do not remember any churchgoing, though there may have been a single attendance at a Sunday School at some point. Of more significance was the racial divide. Our house was on the border of a large run-down black district, and I would stare fascinated at life over the boundary, especially the capacity of men to gob tobacco twenty or thirty yards. I made friends with a black girl who wanted to give me a kitten, but my parents disapproved. We had a black servant, Lena, and my sister and I experienced some distaste at the way my parents talked about her. They were not overtly racist but had imbibed the attitudes of their culture and class. There is enough innocence in a child to sense this and find it uncomfortable.

According to accounts, I arrived back in England in February 1944 as a bright, attractive child with a strong American accent. Our first base was in Cobham, where my grandmother lived at Longridge, Fairmile Lane, and where over the years when my parents were in England, we rented various houses or flats in Cobham. Although my grandmother had an air raid shelter in the garden, we huddled in a cupboard under the stairs as first V1 rockets and then V2s, hit London. Meanwhile there was always New Quay for holidays.

Chapter 3

A bit of Yorkshire

1944–6

It remains a mystery how we landed in Huddersfield, there being no army base nearby that I was aware of. But whatever the reason, we were soon billeted on the Broadbents who, as part of the war effort, agreed to share their house with a military family. Both sides went into the arrangement with some trepidation, my family being very South of England and military, the Broadbents very Yorkshire and business. But my mother and Molly Broadbent got on wonderfully well, and it was the start of a lifetime relationship between the two families. Molly became the godmother of my brother, Charles, who was born in 1945, and when my parents were posted to Singapore I happily stayed with the Broadbents. There were some compensations for the absence of my parents, an attic full of beautifully made lead soldiers, a high quality bow and arrows with its target on the lawn, succulent fruit falling in prodigious quantities from the pear tree and a warm no nonsense mother substitute. Saturday was my day and I could choose what to do. So I collected fish and chips from the local shop in Marsh for lunch, went to watch Huddersfield Town play football in the afternoon and then on to the pictures. One long lasting attachment has been to the football team and the result of the Saturday match is something I look out for eagerly. Huddersfield Town, known then simply as "the town" but later as "the terriers" had been a great team before the War. They won the equivalent of the Premiership three years running, a feat equalled, but not beaten, by Manchester United. After the war they struggled to avoid relegation and dropping from division after another. Then after fifty years

11

they finally climbed back into the Premiership only to drop again two seasons later. Loyal support for Huddersfield Town, with its faded glory, has been a good training for life in the Church of England! Also as talk about football is now about the one common argot, it is a useful bond with so many.

The Broadents had a "works" which during the war made miniature submarines and afterwards washing machines. At home there was roomy comfort and a total lack of pretentiousness. A vivid image is of Molly Broadbent with her ample arms deep in the kitchen sink doing the washing up with a Craven A drooping out of her mouth. The only concessions to luxury were an Alvis in the garage, later changed for a Rolls, two large Airedale dogs and the annual holiday in Scarborough. Brian Broadbent's passion was stamp collecting, so when he returned from work and had finished his supper, he got out his collection and poured over it through his rimless glasses. On Christmas Day when I woke up there was not only a stocking full of gifts but £5 worth of fireworks beside it – a very large amount of money in those days and not something that would have been spent by my careful and less well-off parents. The Christmas period was enlivened by the hilarious stories of Jennifer (later Aebishcher) doing a holiday postal round.

I started at St David's Prep school, walking there past gaunt granite walls to the sound of clanking mills. It was, I think, quite a good little school but the start was traumatic. All the other members of the class were writing away in script and I was still doing block capitals. My handwriting, largely self-taught, has never recovered. I was, however, a reader. The house contained rows of sea stories by Percy F. Westerman.

Church and religion played no part in my time there, though I was glad to learn later that one of my heroes, Owen Chadwick, served his title in Huddersfield before going off to be Chaplain at Wellington College.

Though my time in Huddersfield was short, I am glad that the West Riding has as a result always been part of me. The connection has been kept up not only by support of Huddersfield's football team, but by an Honorary Doctorate from the excellent Huddersfield University. I was glad to be able to confirm Harold Wilson's granddaughters in Oxford and deliver a lecture in his honour as well as, later, an anniversary memorial sermon for him and a tribute at the one for Mary.

At some point I realised that my father had been posted to Singapore and my mother, sister and newly born brother, Charles, would go with him, leaving me alone for three years. And in those days there were no flights for children to see their parents in the holidays. I prayed desperately that they would not have to go. To no avail. So I have an early memory of praying. How did that happen? I think my mother must have taught me to say a child's simple prayer. Although not a churchgoer she had, as mentioned, been sent to a Roman Catholic convent in Belgium and I think something of the faith of the nuns must have rubbed off on her, and from her onto me. So, it seems to me, faith often gets into people before they are aware of it, and the philosophical arguments about it arise later as they become more conscious of it and are at the same time, challenged by some aspect of experience. The prayer did not bring about what I wanted, for my parents duly left me for three years. So whatever the basis of my religion, it is not founded on prayer bringing about what I most wanted. A few times later in life I have prayed for something, eminently good, with equal ardour and desperation, and again then I have had to resign myself to nothing changing for the better, at least in the world of tangible events. Reflection in later years has led me to recognise the real autonomy which God has given to creation in all its aspects. This has forced me to acknowledge that there is a strict limit to what God might do in the way of "interfering" with the regular laws of nature without frustrating his primary purpose. The impersonality of the forces of nature provide an ordered structure on the basis of which we plan for the future and this is an essential condition for the bringing into being of rational minds.

Receiving an honorary doctorate at Huddersfield University, with Bob Cryan, Vice-Chancellor, and Patrick Stewart, Chancellor

Chapter 4

Welsh roots

As mentioned, we had a number of different homes and my parents were abroad leaving me in England for two long periods. Because of this and the fact that New Quay was where I always went for the longer holidays it has been a place of continuity in my life and one to which I look back for my roots. By education and upbringing, I am thoroughly anglicised and am therefore rather a bogus Welshman but I say I would rather be a bogus Welshman than an authentic Englishman and you cannot be more Welsh than that! And although Jo is very English, we are both passionate supporters of Wales at rugby, and not just through the years when they had such great teams. Dylan Thomas lived in Talsarn, just outside New Quay, from 1941–3 and then in New Quay itself from 1944–5 where he drank heavily in the Black Lion. I have never doubted that the main source of inspiration for *Under Milkwood*, which was mainly written before he moved to Laugherne, was New Quay and the detailed research of David N. Thomas has substantiated this through a whole range of detail. My childhood memories of New Quay just before and after World War II have all the atmosphere of the play.[2]

It is New Quay in 1939. The child lay in bed listening to the noises of the night. Wind made the trees restless and gusts agitated the leaves. Bark scraped against bark. Birds and animals and unknown, un-nameable sounds could be heard. It was a little frightening, anxiety-making. Anxiety was in the air for war had been declared and in anticipation of the bombing my mother had left Eltham, a part of London likely to be bombed, to flee West. Perhaps it was the disquiet of the time that made me particularly protective towards our young puppy. I didn't like it when adults were cross about its little puddles.

My Welsh grandfather, Arthur, had retired from Llandeilo to live in New Quay where his wife, Margaret, came from, and whose family had lived in the village for more than 200 years. He lived alone in No 2 Pentregarth, Margaret having died in 1944. When he retired to New Quay, he told his friends in Llandeilo he would come back often to see them but so settled did they become in New Quay he never did in fact make the 30-mile journey back. My parents had number 3 Pentregarth, one of five small, attached cottages.

Grandpa was a well-built, handsome man, with a strong jaw and nose. "One for the ladies", so it was said, though no doubt his ardent non-conformist piety kept him in check most of the time. Certainly, he was sociable and liked to go down to the village to sit on the Green "clonking" i.e., chatting people up. He also liked to do good and his favourite way was through one of his inventions. Much of the time he spent in his little garage opposite No 2 making things. He was famous for his washing machines. These consisted of two baking dishes, one slightly smaller than the other, with holes punched in them and screwed together and fastened on the end of a pole, long or short, with a handle on the end. When clothes were put in a tub the handle was pushed up and down, soapy water gushed in and out of the holes and the general agitation of the clothes washed any dirt away. In short there was a great deal of movement with little expenditure of energy and, above all, the hands were kept dry. These were much in demand. Also useful was a wire bent in such a way as to open windows normally out of reach. Grandpa never threw anything away. Every piece of string or screw was neatly kept in some container on his work bench.

His living habits were similarly economical. It is said that he refused the State Pension on principle and lived on £1 a week from his savings. His diet was invariable: a rice pudding cooked in the stove by the coal fire in the kitchen, bread, cheese, an occasional boiled egg and real coffee.

Talking to a distant cousin of my father, Willie Harries, at Glanmyddyfi, the family farm outside Llandeilo about my grandfather, he said he had been the leader of the "split" – a word in which we have summed up the whole fissiparous history of Welsh non-conformity. In other words, a leading member of the congregation has a row with the minister and ups and offs with half the congregation to build a new chapel nearby. There were many chapels in New Quay and Grandpa settled into the Tabernacle which I attended on one occasion. The minister seemed to take the whole service, including the prayers, with two sermons, one allegedly for children, and the congregation with no vocal part at all except for the reading of the lessons. I can still hear in my mind the reading of the Prologue to St John's Gospel. "In the beginning was the word," there was then as long a pause as I have ever heard in church before the reader continued, "and the word was with God." Similar powerful pauses punctuated the whole reading.

In Grandpa's bathroom were piles of old copies of the *Readers' Digest* and he himself liked to give guidance to the young in a similar crisp style. Grandpa built a seat for people exhausted by the very steep hill on the way up to Pentregarth. On it he wrote "Rest and be thankful". That seat now has a memorial plaque on it to him, a fitting symbol of his practical piety.

Rubbish in those days was collected in a large wooden cart drawn by a horse. Milk, however, was delivered in a motorised vehicle by two ladies in their 20s. I can still feel their warm smiles and cheerful daily greeting. And this is the abiding memory of New Quay in the 1940s – friendliness to children in the shops, on the streets and from our various great aunts, uncles, cousins, second cousins and so on. The people of New Quay genuinely liked and enjoyed children.

New Quay is a key part of my life. As mentioned, it was where I always went for summer holidays and some others. It was where we took our children, and where our children took their children. It has wonderful sandy safe beaches for children and great cliff walks. When I used to stand on the cliffs and look down the coast to Ynys Lochtyn by Llangranog and Cardigan Island, I always used to say to myself, "The best view in Europe and nobody knows about it." Now they do know and it has become a favourite for walkers.

The beaches are where I spent much of my childhood, especially the mile of sand known as Traethgwyn. I like to imagine Dylan Thomas walking back home along the beach from the Black Lion leaving a little of his literary spirit to fall on my child's head. T.S. Eliot used to holiday at the house of his Chairman, Geoffrey Faber, just a few miles inland. There is a photo of him on a beach that I recognise as Traethgwyn, and I like to imagine, even more, something of his spirit falling on me.

When I became a life peer, the Garter King of Arms told me that I would have to have a Nomen dignitatum. Initially I chose "of Ceinewydd" but due to the pressure of my wife I went back to him and got it changed to Pentregarth. People often ask me where it is as they cannot find it on a map, which is not surprising as it is a row of cottages.

In recent years there has been a great deal of discussion about identity. There has also been a growing recognition that we have multiple identities. I regard myself as Christian by religion, Welsh by nationality, British by citizenship and European by culture. So the Welsh strain is only one element, but it is very much there. In 2021, aged 84, I made a resolution to learn Welsh, which, so far, I do every day on Duolingo – a small act of reparation for the loss of the language in my family. Now when I wake up in New Quay and go out of the front door to breathe in the fresh air and the smell of Buddleia and hear the sound of birds, I think of the Reverend Eli Jenkins of *Under*

Milkwood and the prayer he uttered at his front door for those who lived their lives under Milk Wood, to the God he knows will be the first "to see our best side, not our worst".

With grandson Toby, looking south from New Quay to Ynys Lochtyn and Cardigan Island: 'The best view in Europe'.

Chapter 5

Marbles and conkers

1945–9

Haileybury and Imperial Service College, Junior School, in the immediate post-war years could well be likened to the prep school described in Evelyn Waugh's *Decline and Fall*. The masters, for one reason or another, were clearly not fit for military service. The blotched and reddened hands and face of one clearly revealed his alcoholic tendencies, the dark shadow and multiple cuts on the face of another, his inability to control his razor, let alone unruly boys.

As I left for school and said goodbye to my mother she started to cry. Clearly I had to act the man, so held back my own tears in order to comfort her. It was a realistic strategy for adjusting to the new environment. Hold back your tears and get on with it. That's what we all had to do, there being no alternative. Division into gangs was a feature of the school, with some minor torturing of new boys, but nothing excessive. There was no real cruelty in the school, and in the light of what has later been revealed about so many schools at that time, no sexual abuse that I was aware of. The senior boy in my dormitory once called me over to sleep beside him on his bed for a while. Nothing happened other than feeling somewhat embarrassed. The worst aspects were the food and the cold. The winter of 1946/7 was the worst for three centuries and there were widespread food shortages. In the main hall area where we spent a great deal of time there was one small stove round which we huddled if we could. The regular stew with its scraggy, fatty meat and barley literally made me feel sick just to look at it. There were, however, two table delights not often encountered later in life. One was bread and dripping. This was the congealed residue of fat and gravy from the Sunday joint and was a great food for hungry boys. The other was the potatoes that came with the Sunday joint. None of your lightly roasted ones with little fat on them. These were at once well roasted and so squishy that when you pushed them a small geyser of oil spouted up.

It was not a deliberately cruel or perverse regime, nevertheless the ultimate deterrent for indiscipline was caning. We slept in dormitories, and when we were all in bed the headmaster used to come in carrying his cane. The miscreant had to bend over the back of his bed and was caned on the bottom four or six times according to the seriousness of the offence. The headmaster was an ex-golf and hockey blue with strong arms and wrists so it made an impact. I was once part of a riot in my dormitory when we started to throw toothbrushes and so on into some poor boy's pot. I was duly beaten and for months at home had to make sure no one saw the brown weals in case someone asked what they were for.

I can't remember learning anything in the classroom but the pleasures of the playground remain in my mind still. Marbles were our main amusement. Marbles with beautiful colours inside them were highly prized and still the sight of one seems to me like the gold of Ophir. They could be small or large, their value in the game depending both on the size and the elegance of the coloured swirls inside. In contrast to the valuable marbles with their magical twists of colour there were the ordinary bottle green ones which counted for only one. Games with marbles took two forms. In one there was a circle in the dust with marbles placed inside by each of the players. The object was to throw a marble from outside in order to hit one inside and knock it out of the circle. In the other game one player threw their marble and the other person threw theirs after it in order to hit it. A marble of the value of five, for example, had to be hit five times before it was lost or won.

In the autumn marbles was replaced by conkers, now frowned on by health and safety regulators but a source of great delight to us. Each conker was on a string and the object was to swing one's own in such a way as to hit the other person's conker and break it. Conkers that survived had a value according to the number of other conkers it had destroyed. Subtle ways were found of hardening conkers, including baking them so that they could accumulate great value.

Diversions from marbles and conkers were provided by modelling and flying balsa wood gliders, the wealthier boys being able to afford gliders with long wingspans. Also a regular sport was horses and riders, one boy being carried on the shoulders of another. Two horses charged at one another with the riders trying to pull the other off. More sedately, sometimes we played bowls on the lawn under the large Cedar tree.

Sport was a high priority and the source of much enjoyment. I was a stylish bat and went in number one for the school, but had a propensity for getting out for a duck. At rugby I fared rather better, being a smallish, bouncy scrum half. I loved flinging myself forward as I threw the ball from the back of the scrum to the fly half. Once I even threw myself so vigorously into a scrummage that I received an egg sized bump on my forehead.

Outside it was mainly cricket we followed, a great time of success for the England team with star players like Hutton, Washbrook, Edrich and Dennis Compton whose well brushed shiny hair was familiar to the whole country through the Brylcreem advertisement he appeared in. My favourite was Hutton, and my loyalties divided between Yorkshire and Surrey.

In Huddersfield I had passed a grade or two on the piano, with lessons from Molly Broadbent. Lessons at school were taken by a mistress and it was regarded as a rather sissy thing to do, so I managed to avoid ever having one during my first term. In my first holidays before she had gone abroad to join my father, I told her I wanted to give up music. I vividly remember the scene at my grandmother's house, with her at one end of the room and me at the other. "You will regret this to your dying day," she said; which I have.

On Sundays we were walked to church in Windsor. The building was all monuments and flags, and the service a choral Mattins. All of great cultural, historical and patriotic significance no doubt but it did nothing for me religiously. The school, whose address was Clewer Manor, was close by the Clewer Sisters, the religious order that I became Visitor of when I was Bishop of Oxford. They offered a rather different version of Anglicanism but we did not experience it. The school had a chaplain, a slight, thin man with glasses whom I'm afraid we thought of as rather a weed, to use the jargon of the day.

We were cold, the food was not good and the institution was emotionally bleak. But we took comfort from one another. We might even form families with one boy designated as father, another as mother and one as their child. We formed friendships and enjoyed the rough playground activities we did together.

After my first term, when my mother left to join my father in Singapore, it must have felt particularly bleak for me, because I spent the whole term in the san or sanitorium. First I went down with chicken pox and then measles. But I had all the joy of reading a Biggles book a day, exciting stories about a World War I fighter ace. The book shelves in the main hall were lined with heavy volumes by G.A. Henty, which my father encouraged me to read. But I never did. Biggles stories were the ones for me.

At breakfast in the dining room the headmaster and his wife sat at the head of one table. We boys were fascinated by his coffee percolator, watching the water rise up and then fall through the grains into the glass container below. One day at breakfast he called me over. "I'm afraid we are going to have to look for a new scrum half next season," he said. He wanted me to know I had passed the Common Entrance exam for Wellington.

So we see a boy learning to put up with things, developing a capacity to endure, but also with a capacity for fun and friendship in a rather bleak environment and a delight in lighthearted play.

Chapter 6

Pinpricks of light

1949–54

Wellington College at this time was a pretty rough, vulgar and arrogant environment. There was much boasting about masturbation, some talk about crushes of older boys on younger ones and a fair amount of tormenting. There was no sexual abuse that I am aware of but I found much that went on distasteful. When I went back to Wellington as Bishop of Oxford the story told there was that I had been unhappy at school. That is not quite correct. If you had asked me at the time, I would have said I was very happy, thank you. For in those days when you were asked how things were you of course replied, "Fine, thanks" and talked about the latest rugby match. In retrospect I see now I was not as happy as I then suggested I was. Since then the reputation of the school has risen hugely, especially through Sir Anthony Seldon, who introduced "happiness" to the curriculum, amongst other things. When I spoke to him not long after he took over as Master (headmaster) he told me he had two ambitions for Wellington, "To make it a great school – again," and "to make it an interesting school, most schools are so dull." By all accounts he succeeded, making it at the time the most sought after school in the country and certainly the most talked about.

I was happy enough ragging around with my friends. A fair amount of teasing and setting on people went on, and in the light of later attitudes I can remember seeing the one Jewish boy in my house being tormented as Jewish, and finding it somehow different and unpleasant. Caning by both prefects and tutors went on: a terrifying piece of theatre. The dormitory consisted of a long corridor with horseboxes up each side, each boy having this minimum of half private space. We would all be in bed, everything deadly quiet, and footsteps would be heard walking up the centre of the dormitory followed by a knock on some boy's door. Then there would be the swish of the cane, the number of swishes being heard and counted in every room. Fagging also went on. I was fag to D.C.K. Watson, later well known and much loved as an early leader of the Charismatic movement in the Church of England. He was Head of House and Head of College, and went on to read philosophy at Cambridge. I remember him as an exceedingly nice and sensitive person even before he became a well-known Christian.

What went on in the classroom at that time is a fog in my memory, no doubt caused by a mixture of boredom and daydreaming. Novels, however, were a great solace. Most nights our tutor went round the dormitory to ask boys how they were getting on. When he came into my room he always found me having gone to bed early reading a novel. His invariable comment was, "My boy, why aren't you working?" I later wrote in the introduction to my book *Haunted by Christ: modern writers and the struggle for faith*,[3] that the book was a result of "not working". My reading matter at that time consisted of good middle brow novels like the Hornblower series by C.S. Forrester, Daphne Du Maurier and in later teenage years, Thomas Hardy. I read Richard Llewellyn's *How Green Was My Valley*, about a rugby playing Welsh mining community, three times straight through, no sooner finishing than going back to the beginning. I suspect that this helped to create my desire to have a Welsh identity.

Another highlight was the visit of a Canadian High School drama group who put on a performance of Thornton Wilder's *Our Town*. My Tutor was big on the new American musicals, which went down well with most boys. I enjoyed them but nothing made the impact of that theatre production. With just a few hard backed chairs as props, the life of a small town was conjured into existence by good acting. I was totally captivated. It corresponded with my ideal of theatre, as expressed by Peter Brook in his book *The Empty Space,* which I read in later years, and instilled in me the seed of a lifelong love of the theatre.

Early on I took the female lead in a production of *Nothing but the Truth.* (A 1941 production had starred Bob Hope.) I gather I did rather well. But my tutor wrote to my parents to say that it had gone to my head and resulted in poor work. In fact, the cause of this was rather different. Playing the female lead brought about a fair amount of unkind teasing. Anyway, at some point my work was so poor I was put back a year. I have no doubt it was due to the secret misery of that period.

After I left Wellington, I learnt that my tutor had been an alcoholic and that he had burned himself to death in a laboratory. Clearly not a happy man. When he left I had a new tutor, Bobby Moss, who seemed to think that this rather ordinary boy did have some promise. At least when my father announced that he was taking me away from school early he expressed disappointment and said he had wanted me to be head of house. In later years I have always been keen to remind teachers what a difference they can make to a child by believing in them rather than making them feel a failure.

A change of tutor coincided with a surprising sporting success. Any early promise I had as a rugby player at prep school rapidly disappeared when I started to grow lanky as a teenager, not heavy enough for the scrum and not quick enough to be the good three quarters I aspired to be. But on holidays in Catterick, where my father had been posted, I was out with the beagles and discovered that running across fields was rather invigorating. Next term at school, in the house team for the annual Bigside race, expecting to come way down the field as usual, I found myself in the top few and in the school team. Deciding to do a little training, I then found myself winning the Kingsley, another big school race but over tougher country, including crossing a river, by a large margin. So this sporting success, with an affirmative house tutor who believed in me, meant that I left college with morale high.

Religion consisted of daily morning prayer. This meant in effect switching off when one went into the chapel and switching on again on leaving. The chaplain, a genial man, took R.E. lessons. These consisted of him spending most of the time carefully drawing the journeys of St Paul on the blackboard in coloured chalk. I think I obtained about 20% in my School Certificate. But one boy scored zero, and the school were stopped taking the exam. We were expected to be confirmed. Interviewed by my tutor about this, he asked, "Have you looked into the other religions, Buddhism for example?" "Yes, sir," I replied, though I had hardly heard the word Buddhism before. But duly confirmed I was, and took it seriously to the extent I knew something was expected of me. Once a week there was a voluntary Communion service in the evening and I remember going once or twice. It provided a place of peace, a touch of what later I would think of as "the peace which passeth all understanding". My experience leads me to want to take adolescent religion seriously, however simple and uninformed. Also to think that what matters are small, simple, practical steps.

The ethos of such schools as Wellington, though often set up on firm Christian grounds, is not conducive to the development of serious faith. This has been even more so in recent decades, geared up as they are to obtain the kind of exam success that leads to good universities and good jobs in the City, for which parents are paying such large sums of money. I once went back and preached on the concept of service, stressing that this did not necessarily mean you had to become a social worker or work in overseas aid, it could be expressed in many professional occupations. Afterwards two boys sauntered up to me and said, "Very interesting, Sir, but of course we don't think like that here."

So, did I have faith at Wellington? and what, if anything, was present that might have nurtured it to flower later? I must have had an instinctive faith that, as mentioned earlier, seems to have rubbed off from my mother. For I can remember when one friend, who had somehow managed to buy a bulk load of contraceptives to sell, announced that there was no God, I found myself protesting that there was. But it was totally unthought through. I can also remember poking my head above a pew one morning in chapel and looking around and thinking to myself, "This is not what Jesus meant, not what he meant at all." So there must have been something there, however minimal. It amused me later in life to see that this phrase, with its cadences, was used in *The Love Song of J. Alfred Prufrock*.

Two other memories remain relevant to my later turn to faith. One is of two members of staff kneeling devoutly for a short period after the formal prayers in chapel. They were very different, one at the centre of a coterie of bright historians, who later tried his hand at being a monk, the other a scientist who was totally hopeless at keeping discipline in class. Strange that I should remember this apparently insignificant detail. Was it the prayers of a few faithful souls that later bought forth fruit in some of the boys including me?

The other memory is of the Master (Headmaster) reading the scripture passage for Thursday morning assembly, which on that day of the week was held in the memorial hall rather than the chapel. Harry House the Master, who had been much decorated for bravery in World War I had come to the headship from the civil service, and apparently did not get on well with the staff. He was the least eloquent of men, who could not utter two words without the sound "uh", so he was known as "uh,uh, House". But I can still feel the great intensity with which he read 1 Corinthians 13, which he often did. It was as though all the terrible carnage of the war, and the unhappiness of the staffroom had focussed his faith on the words "Now abideth, faith, hope charity and the greatest of all is charity."

So, nothing in the way of serious faith when I left Wellington but, in retrospect, a few apparently unimportant details that left an impression; a few pinpricks of light.

Ice-skating with my mother and brother, Charles.

Chapter 7

On time and in good order

1954–6

My father took me away from school early so he could get me started on a career in the army as soon as I was 18, without wasting time. So, I had some tutorials in Catterick with staff from the Royal Army Education Corps to prepare for the equivalent of today's A-levels, played lots of golf, fell in love with Jennie Williamson (later Speed), and obtained some indifferent grades. I then went straight into doing the necessary 10 weeks basic training also at Catterick, as a prelude to going to Sandhurst. Why the army? Wellington sent a lot of people into the army at that time, there was nothing else I was drawn to, and the army offered a salary at a young age with plenty of sport.

My father was Commandant of the Signals Training Brigade, which at the time consisted of 9 training regiments. National Service was in full swing and one regiment, which had a Major who spent his whole time scouring Rugby league clubs for talent, had a team of international standard. Life in the ranks was pretty brutal and a great leveller. It did, however, have one great blessing. It meant that at that time, when virtually every male in the country had to do two years military service, there was a shared experience which provided a common culture and language amongst men rarely seen before and not at all since.

Having a father who was commandant had one advantage. He arranged for those of us who were doing their basic training before going to Sandhurst to do a week's driving course at Ripon. We drove solidly for seven days, took the exam and all failed. So the course was extended for two days, we took the exam again and passed. It qualified me to drive not only cars, but motorbikes and three-ton trucks. Those were the days when driving lorries, in particular, you had to double declutch. You had to develop a perfect sense of timing in order to declutch before engaging the gears again. Very satisfying when you got it right and a terrible grinding noise when you didn't.

One day when we were firing away in the very noisy indoor range there was a sudden hush as the shooting stopped. Some mildly critical remarks of mine about Sergeant Bateman who was in charge, floated into the silence. Proceedings were brought to a rapid halt as I was marched up against a wall. The sergeant, with his big moustache close to my face, slowly looked me up and down and coldly enunciated, "You bloody bastard of a Brigadier's son, I am putting you on a charge for inciting a mutiny." A rather speedy and dramatic end to my military career, I thought. But he must have relented, for somehow I went on to Sandhurst a few weeks later. I can see Sergeant Bateman's face when by chance I passed him on Darlington Station on my way there. The world is not fair.

The unwritten policy at Sandhurst was to break cadets down and then build them up again in its own image of what an officer and gentleman should be like. The main objective for the cadet in the early weeks was to avoid being noticed as being dozy or sloppy in any way. There was much shouting and quick fire questioning. "Parade is at 7 am, what time will you be at the parade, Sir?" "7 am, Sergeant" "Wrong, five minutes to seven. Don't let me catch you being dozy, again, Sir." Later as an underofficer, practising sword drill on the playground at 6.30 am, one of us was rather slow, so the fiery Irish Sergeant Major berated us with the words, "The first thing an officer must learn, Sirs, is to take his drink." However late the night before, we had to be there next morning ready to do a professional job.

So the first thing I learned at Sandhurst was to be on parade, well on time, and in good order. It meant I have always been able to get dressed in a matter of seconds and have tended to catch not one but two trains before the one I could well have caught.

I was young enough to take Sandhurst on its own terms, which basically was to work hard and play hard. I ran for the Academy on the track in the summer and over the country in winter. This meant that I missed all the military law lectures which took place on Saturday mornings when as often as not I would be travelling to an away fixture. When the final exams came round, I got hold of some old papers, spotted the questions likely to come up and won the military law prize. I still have the leather-bound volume I was given, a history of the Dreyfus case.

A temptation avoided at Sandhurst was to get beguiled into being commissioned into one of the smart regiments, rather than the Royal Signals, which was not very fashionable but which offered a better prospect of going to university and a long-term career. I enjoyed the company of my friends going into the smart regiments, and in particular the insouciance and understatement of the Brideshead world. They would drive up to London night clubs and then back for parade next morning. One, about to have a bad smash remarked just before the two cars hit, "This is going to be expensive." When we passed out from Sandhurst, the three or four hundred of us were listed in order of merit, based partly on academic work and partly on officer qualities. I passed out rather high, as did my friend John Magnay, going into the Grenadier Guards. He rang his father to tell him the good news, only to receive the reply that it was not done for Grenadiers to pass out so high! There was much celebrating in the last week or so because of this success, with a fair amount of drinking and rampaging. The sensible Major in charge of our company took John Magnay and myself aside and in the nicest possible way told us to cool it and not ruin everything by going too far, which we already had.

Religion played no obvious part in my time there but there was a service of Holy Communion at 7 am on some weekday mornings. It coincided with the time of parade and offered a less stressful alternative. I think I must have gone once or twice, probably because I did not feel I was in good enough order for going on parade. By such thin threads the good Lord holds us. But I think it must have been at Sandhurst that a strange statement suddenly appeared in my mind. "If Christianity is true it had better be at the centre of my life. If it is untrue better to give it up altogether." I made no immediate response but it was a seed that later began to germinate.

So duly kitted out from my clothing allowance, not just with uniforms but a beautiful country suit, a trilby and a British Warm from the best tailors and outfitters in the St James area, I was duly commissioned into the Royal Signals at the beginning of 1956 and went to Catterick for a young officers' course.

As a Junior Under Officer at Sandhurst in 1955.

Chapter 8

An inner volcano

1956–8

The young officers' course was followed by a few months as part of the vast army we then maintained in Germany, the British Army of the Rhine (BAOR). It consisted of 80,000 personnel, the same number as the whole British Army today. I was attached to a Brigade Signals Squadron at Minden in Germany. This was an interesting posting, because being at Brigade HQ responsible for communication to the companies in the Brigade, you knew what was going on. Much of the summer we spent out on exercise on the North German plains. The cold war was at its height, and in 1956 Soviet troops entered Hungary to suppress the October revolution. In the same year the autobahns were filled with endless convoys of British trucks on the move as part of the response to the Suez crisis.

I lived alone in the officers mess with the servants all to myself. When I arrived, the Intelligence officer went on holiday and asked me to look after his Mercedes car, his horse and his two dogs. All this at scarcely twenty.

After another period in Catterick to prepare for and take the Mechanical Sciences Qualification Exam, Part I, for entrance to Cambridge, I went out to Germany again to serve with a Heavy Radio Relay troop in Dusseldorf. This involved commanding what were called "hairy arsed linesman" as they rolled out very thick BICC cable, as part of the communications network back to Army Headquarters to what was then spelled München Gladback. Although I served as a regular army officer I fought no fiercer enemy than the soot in the Ruhr Valley and the wind in Catterick.

Life was pleasant and I did a fair amount of running for the regiment and the BAOR including a trip to Berlin for an Athletics event.

As mentioned in the preface, it was during this couple of years that something happened that changed my whole life. The thought that had come into my mind about Christianity, that if it was true it ought to be central to my life, started to work its effect. I seemed to gravitate to friends for whom the Christian faith was important, one who had trained for ordination and who had dropped out a week before and who went into the army instead; another, an ex-art student who had wanted to be ordained but had not been selected and an evangelical ordinand doing National Service who was due to go on to Cambridge. At the same time, I started to read around the faith. I even very occasionally went to a weekday service of Holy Communion in one of the regimental chapels in Catterick. A small step but if you are not used to it, to go to a service as one of the only two or three people present means overcoming certain inner barriers of embarrassment and shyness.

Insights came from strange quarters. One day in Germany I was reading Aldous Huxley's *Perennial Philosophy*. The thesis of this book is that at the heart of all the great religions of the world is the imperative of self-giving and the truth that we find ourselves by giving ourselves away. It struck me that if this was a widely shared moral truth it was rooted in a spiritual truth about the nature of ultimate reality and the sharpest focus of this was the Christian claim that God gives himself to us to the extent of becoming one with us. The truth of the incarnation suddenly seemed to be the living focus of a wider truth.

A continuous source of insight was provided by Lance Corporal John Haliburton. John had done a degree at Cambridge and was doing National Service before going back to study at Theological College. He was the most unsoldierly person in the regiment, with a shaggy baggy battle dress and a waddling walk. But not much in regiment happened without him. He ran the regimental office, was the regimental interpreter, ran the regimental dance band, the chapel, the Bible study group and played the organ for services. Late one night when I was patrolling the barracks on Orderly Officer duty I saw a small light on in one room. I went to find out what it was and discovered John Haliburton reading Owen Chadwick's latest book, *From Bossuet to Newman,* a book about the development of doctrine. When he was not doing any of these things, John Haliburton used to sneak into the Officers mess and in return for my sherry talk theology to me. Sadly, we later came to disagree over the ordination of women.

One day some months earlier, in the library in Catterick, probably looking for a novel by Hardy or Balzac, I picked up a book of essays by Roman Catholic priests on why they had been ordained. I took it home and read it and thought, "Wouldn't it be funny if one day I was ordained." It is a mystery why I picked up the book and why I should have had that thought, because it was very far from the way I was actually planning my life. I was all set to go to Cambridge to read Mechanical Sciences, and religion still played a rather minor role in my life. However, as stated earlier, over the next few months the thought recurred from time to time. "Wouldn't it be funny if one day you were ordained." Then serving in Germany mentally preparing myself for Cambridge I thought to myself, "Wouldn't it be nice when I retire from the army as a General with a good pension to spend my life as a country parson." Then, smack, bang, another thought came. "Well, if that is what you are meant to be doing, you had better do it now." An inner volcano exploded.

I never experienced a violent conversion to the Christian faith. Rather it gradually seeped into me, drew me and then firmly took hold of me. There is a line in *The Cloud of Unknowing,* a fourteenth-century mystical work, later quoted by T. S. Eliot in *The Four Quartets,* which beautifully and succinctly sums up what happened to me over a period of 18 months or so. "The drawing of this love and the voice of this calling", I was drawn by this love and responded to this calling. It strengthened in the call not just to be a serious Christian with the faith at the centre of my life but in the conviction that I was meant to be ordained. Not for one moment have I regretted it.

It was very strange. To repeat what I wrote earlier, no clergyman had ever been a role model. In fact just the opposite. The chaplain at my prep school struck me as a weed. The chaplain at Wellington was genial but I did not know him and he did not spiritually attract me. There were no clergy in my family. Moreover, I had no experience of ordinary church life as a member of a congregation. My family had not gone to Church when I was a young boy and later I was away from home. I can indeed remember the one solitary time we did indeed go to church as a family when we were living at Cobham. The Vicar of the neighbouring village of Stoke d'Abernon had a reputation as a good preacher, so my parents decided to go one Sunday and took me with them. I found the sermon an unbearable piece of ham acting. So there was absolutely nothing about the clergy or church life to attract me, indeed I had no experience of parish life. I certainly wouldn't even be put forward for a selection conference these days. However, a CACTM selection conference as it was then called was quickly arranged. I had been brought up to look a person in the eye and be confident, so when the presiding bishop asked me whether I believed I had been called to ordination I duly answered "Yes" and was recommended. And I did believe it.

Back in New Quay on holiday after this as I was walking down the street, I passed the grocers shop that always smelled of a mixture of bacon and furniture polish when the owner, Maurice Williams, emerged from the gloom at the back out into the street to clasp me by the hand. "Oh, Richard," he said "I'm so glad to hear you've got a calling." Three times he repeated it, each time holding my hand tightly and pumping my arm up and down. "Oh, I'm so glad to hear you've got a calling." And I was glad too. If you had asked me what I thought I was called to do, I think I probably had a picture in my mind of knocking on the doors of some drab street in a grey Northern town bringing light and comfort to those inside. Where this idea came from I have no idea. I had no role model in which it featured. What it seems to indicate is that I thought people's lives could be transformed and made much happier if they could see there was a real purpose in human life. I wanted them to see that the Christian faith gives us meaning and joy.

When I told my parents my plans, they were pretty horrified, having got me off their hands with my future settled. They had no inkling of the churning up that had been going on inside me. Later they understood and were hugely supportive. Officially an officer had to serve for five years after Sandhurst but ordination was one of the reasons why this rule might be relaxed, and the Queen was graciously pleased to let me go. I later heard that someone who left for this reason was found rubber planting in Malaya, but my call remained firm. I had this place at Cambridge to read engineering but when I told the college I wanted to read theology instead I lost it as they did not admit theology students. So I wrote around a simple letter to a number of colleges explaining my situation and Selwyn kindly had mercy on me. It was all so much easier in those days. But I had no money. If I had gone up on the army I would have had everything paid for me and received a full salary. When I applied as a civilian for a county grant, I was refused on the grounds that my parents should pay. But understandably they declined, having launched me into the world. So I went up to Cambridge with no money except a £100 Kitchener Scholarship. I took up the issue with my local MP, a man whose views I would certainly later reject, who kindly took up my case and eventually ensured that I was judged independent of my parents and therefore eligible for a full grant. With a brick laying job for some of the summer and a Christmas post round it was enough to live on comfortably without getting into debt. So different from today's poor students.

Giving up a settled future and going up to university with no money on the basis of a very recent and untried sense of vocation can only be described as headstrong and imprudent by an older cautious mind. But it did not seem like that to me at the time. Like Martin Luther "I could do no other". It was not a choice: something powerful had taken hold of me. I felt hugely excited.

Chapter 9

Carefree years

1958–61

So it was that with a group of friends also studying theology at Selwyn College, Cambridge, I tried to absorb some ancient near Eastern history, the Old and New Testaments, Hebrew, Greek, and Philosophy of Religion. The biggest intellectual influence on my time at Cambridge was the Scottish philosopher Donald MacKinnon, whose eccentricity was legendary. One story had it that at a dinner party when one speaker was going on too long he crawled under the table and bit his leg. I once visited him at his home in my capacity as secretary of the Theological Society. After letting me in, he continued to pace up the room muttering to himself about whether Jesus lusted after women and wondering what were the implications of him being truly human. MacKinnon had a large head, with bulbous eyes. As he began a sentence, his eyes looking heavenwards, he raised his hands, each clasped round a finely sharpened pencil. Then the rest of the sentence would come out with something of a rush and his hands would come down. The pencils, point down, would stop just short of being smashed into the podium. Then he would stop, pace the room a couple of times and begin another sentence again in the same manner. It was the best theatre in Cambridge. It certainly defied the old definition of a lecture being the notes of the lecturer passing to the notes of the student without going through the brains of either. We experienced a man trying to think his way through some of philosophy's most testing questions.

He influenced us in four main ways. First, he never let us forget that we live in a world of manifest evil.[4] We had to face up to the existence of the Holocaust, nuclear weapons

41

and many unspeakable cruelties. Secondly, he drew widely on the whole field of human culture, not least Greek tragedy. Thirdly, against the popular trend at the time he argued that the Christian faith was committed to making statements about the way things really are, about alleged facts. When a Christian says something about God or Christ he or she is making an assertion that something is the case. This meant that for him the Christian faith was closer to Marxism than philosophical idealism, because it was concerned with events, not just ideas. He was committed to what my friend, the scholar John Drury has described as "brute facticity". One implication of this was that he argued that the tomb of Jesus really was found empty, and he took part in a famous debate with Professor Geoffrey Lampe who held the opposite view, namely that the essence of the resurrection of Christ was to be found in the appearance stories, not the empty tomb, which was a later rationalisation. One of the results of the influence of Donald MacKinnon on me was that I was unimpressed later by the philosophy in John Robinson's book *Honest to God* which created such a furore in the 1960s. I did think that that book served a useful pastoral and spiritual purpose in helping people to rediscover God in their own lives but its theological framework seemed to me inadequate. Due to MacKinnon's influence, I still think we have to answer the question as to whether something is or is not the case.

Donald MacKinnon's inaugural lecture was titled "The Borderlands of Theology" and its argument was that today the Christian thinker has to exist on the border between faith and the wider culture, feeling the incursions of that culture into its own territory. That has been absolutely fundamental to my own ministry whether in a parish or university context and is the fourth way in which he was a major influence on me. I am not someone who works at the academic coalface. I have neither the aptitude, temperament or scholarly apparatus for that.

What I have tried to do is relate the Christian faith to the wider culture of literature, the arts, ethics, politics and other religions. I try to do my thinking on that interface, on the borderlands in MacKinnon's terms.

At that time in philosophy logical positivism had given way to linguistic analysis, but some of the assumptions behind logical positivism still reigned. For those of us doing philosophy of religion it focussed on whether Christian statements did in fact have any meaning at all. It was argued that a bold assertion such as "God loves the world" seems so incompatible with the world of suffering we know that "it dies the death of a thousand qualifications". As we got into this world of linguistic analysis we felt the basic Christian beliefs slipping through our fingers into meaninglessness. It was a healthy challenge and it made us forever aware of the difficulty of all religious language, and what language about the divine can and cannot do. I continue to be highly aware of the problem of using any human words about God.

I did my tutorials with Howard Root, who also directed us to the challenge posed by Camus. Root suggested that the Christian is like the detective in a good crime story. All the evidence seems to point in one direction but the clever detective has noticed other facts, overlooked by the others, which put a different interpretation on events. All the evidence seems to point against there being a loving God, but the Christian has a conviction, based on Jesus, that the true story is very different.

Time passed very happily. I played squash and tennis and socialised. In the trial for the University Cross Country Team, the group I was with were directed the wrong way, so I failed to finish in the first few and decided not to pursue running seriously. But we had an excellent college team of four which included one international (Bruce Tulloch, who had found fame by running in the Olympics bare foot) and one near international. We won a number of events, including one big national one. Selwyn at the time was an under endowed small college geographically on the edge of the university, but an extremely happy place in which to be. In later years some of the main university departments have been built right up to the college grounds, so it now seems almost at the centre of things; and one year recently Selwyn was even top of the academic league table.

When not writing essays for tutorials or going to lectures to do with the course we were studying, we played at being scholars, even learning some Aramaic at one point, and going to other lectures just for the enjoyment of it, such as Owen Chadwick's on the Oxford Movement.

Long vocations were spent on the continent touring in the A40 owned by the mother of my friend Derek Watson. Going with Derek, John Greenhalge and Malcolm Stonestreet, I devoured the museums and galleries of France, Italy and Spain setting up a lifelong love of the arts.

Religion was important in the Cambridge of the time. The Vicar of the University Church was Mervyn Stockwood, a large character who was a formidable debater at the Union in defence of both the Christian faith and socialism. When after his retirement as Bishop of Southwark, a friend rang up and told him a newspaper was going to do an exposé of gay bishops and he was on the list, Mervyn simply replied, "Tell them I've had a lot of women too." On Sunday evenings the University Church had dialogues with national figures like Malcolm Muggeridge which attracted crowds of 1500. There had in fact been a small uplift in the religious life of the nation after World War II, one sign of a new seriousness that had developed during the war. Ordinations into the Church of England rose to nearly 800 a year. I thought I had a vocation from God, and now I find I was just part of a social trend! The Christian Union was strong and a number of people were converted to an evangelical form of the faith who later made a big impact in the Church of England such as David Sheppard, the former England cricket captain and outstanding Bishop of Liverpool and John Habgood, the intellectual Archbishop of York. I was not attracted to this form of the Christian Faith but equally some aspects of Anglo-Catholicism at the time seemed somewhat outré. So together with John Selwyn Gummer (later a prominent Conservative politician and later ennobled as Lord Deben) we founded a Selwyn Branch of the Church Union designed to present a Catholic form of Anglicanism with an intellectual cutting edge to students. We later came to disagree over the ordination of women and he became a Roman Catholic. I was mainly happy to worship in our college chapel, occasionally going to Little St Mary's, one of the Anglo Catholic churches, or St Benet's.

The two main spiritual influences on me were my tutor John Sweet, and the Master of Selwyn, Owen Chadwick. John Sweet taught New Testament and tutored theology students at Cambridge the whole of his working life with great care and patience. Half way through a morning with him, if very exasperated, he would sigh and say, "Oh, dear, I think we had better break for coffee." On Sundays for the 8 am service of Holy Communion, he used to preach a literally one-minute sermon – very telling it was too, and a good model for us all.

Owen Chadwick was a legend. When captaining Cambridge at Rugby, the team got out of hand and wrecked a train, so he as captain accepted responsibility and was sent down. He also played for England in a war time international. He still obtained a first and later became a distinguished academic, Vice Chancellor of the University and heaped with honours. He managed to combine this with being a very holy man. It was a privilege to be with him when he celebrated the Holy Communion in the little upper room above the chapel which was used on weekdays. A number of his phrases still echo in the mind. "Melchizedek brought forth bread and wine, and he was a priest of the most high God" was one such scriptural verse he liked to use at this Communion service. I had a personal link with him as one of my aunts, Joanna Bathurst Brown, was related to Ruth his wife. More significant was the fact that he used to go on Rugby tours with the father of Jo, who later became my wife, and when they stayed with her grandmother in Newcastle, even slept in the same bed. He had a wonderful self-deprecating sense of humour but nevertheless I always found him a bit daunting. His depths seemed to expose my shallowness.

I had obtained a 2.I in Part I of the Tripos and there was talk of getting a first in part II, but in the end only a dull 2.II, probably let down by my Greek, as I suspect I did well on the Philosophy of Religion. But I did not care a fig and I comfort myself with the thought that a whole range of other people like John Henry Newman did equally disappointingly. I had met Jo and we lived the last weeks in a haze. We danced to a steel band through the streets of Cambridge in the small hours after a May Ball then out on the river on a punt early in the morning. We heard *The Dream of Gerontius* together. I had been introduced to Jo early in my time by a friend who had been at Benenden with her, but only properly met up when a Selwyn friend found he had invited two people to the May Ball and asked me whether I would like to take one of them, Jo, as it turned out. She was this rather dreamy lovely looking girl wandering round Girton with a book of poems by Tagore in her hand, a love of whose poems we have always shared.

Within a few days of all this happening we became engaged. In recent years once when I was helping Jo, she grumbled that I was being impatient with her. (This was unusual, for she never normally grumbles, having in recent years developed an extraordinarily equable temperament.) When I protested, she said, "You are very lucky to have me!", with which I agree.

Immediately after we came down Jo was due to go to the Middle East, and especially to Persia, with a group of friends for a couple of months. She had belonged to a prayer group that specially prayed for the tiny Christian church in Persia and indeed had thought of becoming a medical missionary there. I was taken to meet her parents for the first time and when I broached the subject of marrying their daughter, Jo's father replied, "I don't see what this has got to do with going to Persia." Understandably this had all been a bit sudden for them.

Chapter 10

Formation

1961–3

After Cambridge I was due to go to McGill University in Canada on a scholarship. But having become engaged to Jo so soon after we had properly met, it did not seem sensible to conduct a long engagement across the Atlantic; so, plans to go to Canada were scrapped and I re-applied to go to Cuddesdon Theological College where in fact I had first thought of going.

The previous principal of Cuddesdon, under whom I had originally been accepted, Edward Knapp Fisher, was an ascetic man who spent his summer holidays helping out on a local farm. The story has it that one day when he arrived early in chapel for personal prayer he found two students there before him. The next day he arrived earlier still and was first on that occasion, but the following day when he arrived he discovered that the two students had again got there before him; and so the leap frogging went on. (Later Edward Knapp Fisher married and became Bishop of Pretoria.) When Bob Runcie arrived as Principal, the few married students were still not allowed to keep their wives in the vicinity and the presence of women was generally discouraged. They were, however, allowed into the Common Room for half an hour after the Sunday Eucharist for coffee when presumably it was thought the grace of the sacrament would keep the lusts of the young men down, whilst the lusts of the women had not even been thought of at that time.

Luckily the college was very full and I had to be boarded out at one of the farms in the village, with the lovely Palmers. It meant that Jo, who was completing her medical training at University College Hospital in London could visit the farm. Her father had given her a new light blue MG sports car for her birthday, the most elegant design of all their sports cars. She used to come sweeping into the college, long hair flowing in the wind, crunching the gravel in the drive. Both car and girl were much envied.

Cuddesdon had been founded as a result of the Oxford movement and stood for a firm but unfussy spirituality. Prayer and the daily offices were at the heart of its life. It was a good foundation. The staff (Lionel Wickham, Anthony Bird, Peter Cornwall and John Rushton) were all very different and brought varied gifts to the task. The Principal, Princeps as he was called, was Bob Runcie, later Bishop of St Albans and Archbishop of Canterbury. He was very fond of Jo, and I got to know him quite well over the years. He was a great human being, with an unrivalled capacity for honing in on the wavelength of the most diverse range of people. A high point for many at Cuddesdon were the Pastoralia lectures he gave towards the end of their time there. I write more about Bob Runcie in a later chapter on the seven Archbishops of Canterbury I have known.

Having got a degree in Theology I was exempt from a good number of papers of the Ordination exam. It was before the time when people in my position would have been encouraged to begin postgraduate work, so I had more time available than many. Part of this I spent doing a year's placement at Littlemore Mental Health Centre. The chaplain, who was also a medical doctor gave us supervised sessions with patients. This was invaluable experience, for in a parish you meet a range of mental health issues, and my time in the hospital taught me not to be frightened of it, and also to realise the limitations of what a merely pastoral approach could achieve. It was also invaluable when Jo started to have what are now called bipolar episodes.

Littlemore, like most mental health hospitals in those days, was a vast Victorian building in which a good number of patients had spent decades of their life and become institutionalised.

One lady, for example, still thought of herself as Queen Victoria. One huge change for the better has been the advent of modern drugs which has made it possible even for people with serious illnesses to stay out of hospital for much of the time and then when they are ill, to be treated in much smaller institutions.

Two major influences on my time at Cuddesdon were Austin Farrer and Bill Vanstone. Austin Farrer, described as the one genius produced by the Church of England in the twentieth century delivered the Holy Week lectures one year. He shuffled up the aisle, a small, diminutive figure, spoke quietly as if to God for an hour and then slipped away again. He spoke on the atonement in a way that I found answered many half-formulated questions in my mind. He has continued to influence me by his writings throughout my ministry.[5] The paradox about Farrer is that although he wrote scholarly books in both the philosophy of religion and New Testament scholarship, it was in the more popular writings towards the end of his life that his genius flourished. This genius consisted of a unique amalgam of an acutely analytical philosophical mind together with a deep spirituality and a capacity with words that lifted some of his prose into poetry.

Bill Vanstone obtained a string of first class degrees but resisted all offers to go into academic life. Instead, he had spent nearly all his life on a working-class housing estate-at the same time continuing to think deeply about the basis of his Christian beliefs and how they related to human life. He gave a series of lectures at Cuddesdon in which a profound theology was expressed in a series of vivid examples from parish life. These lectures were an early outing for what later became a classic book.[6]

There was my work at the hospital, a little preaching and some study for the ordination exam papers I had to sit, but I still had time available to read more widely, and this meant mainly

George Eliot and Dostoevsky at that time; the latter especially has been a lifelong interest and influence.

The vast majority of students at Cuddesdon were decent, godly men who went on to have faithful ministries as parish priests. We were formed to say our prayers and respond to diverse pastoral needs. But in the light of changes in the wider world, and in particular the cultural cataclysm of the 1960s, we were probably not challenged enough intellectually or in other ways to respond to the rapidly changing, very different cultural landscape. Bob Runcie was conscious of the great weight of Cuddesdon tradition and moved very cautiously. My own time on the staff of a Theological College a few years later made me much more aware of those challenges.

Theological colleges can be very difficult for some students. They are hardly a normal community, formed as they are of people who think that God is calling them to a lifetime of fulltime service. But I had the counterweight of an engagement to Jo and also a capacity to withdraw if things became unbearable. I remember one Good Friday getting so frustrated by the tone and content of the Three Hour addresses, I simply took myself off to the bottom of a field, lay down in the grass and read Paul Tillich's *The Courage to Be,* which helped me through.

The most dreaded ordeal was the college sermon which each student had to preach once during their time there to the college as a whole. After the sermon everyone went back to the common room and in due order each was asked to give their opinion of it. Person after person gave mine a thumbs down, saying they couldn't understand what it was about. I remain eternally grateful when towards the end just one fellow student did get up and give it full approval, saying it was perfectly clear, understandable and relevant to our ministry.

Chapter 11

A pleasant part of the Lord's vineyard

1963–9

I was made Deacon at St Paul's Cathedral at Michaelmas 1963, and a year later was priested there. I was to serve my title at St John's, the handsome eighteenth-century church set in the midst of a row of elegant eighteenth-century houses at the heart of Hampstead. I had thought of myself going to a parish in a rougher area where the Anglicanism was rather more Catholic, but Jo and I were warmed by the family life of the Vicar, Ele Hall, his wife, Pat Hall, and their children, Ricki and Liz. Very importantly it fitted well with Jo doing her House jobs as a young doctor down the road at the Whittington Hospital. We lived at 1, Hollybush Vale, just behind the Everyman Cinema in the middle of the school playground, so with children round us at the front, and overlooking the graveyard at the back we were nicely pitched between the living and the dead.

Some training vicars are martinets, laying down strict rules about the number of pastoral visits to be undertaken each day and checking up on everything that the curate might do. Ele Hall was the opposite. He assumed I was a gentleman and would simply get on with the job as best I thought fit. We met once a week to arrange practical matters but only once did he offer any guidance, when he told me that he thought my standard of preaching had dropped and he would like me to spend more time on preparing sermons and less on doing other things. It was a regime of liberty that I appreciated.

Ele Hall had once been more high church than he later became because he had been badly hurt earlier when he had been Vicar of an Anglo-Catholic church and had reacted against that form of Anglicanism. The result was that at Hampstead he did not fit the bill for the more Catholic members of the congregation, and he had to be fiercely defended by his attractive and able wife, Pat. People project all kinds of fantasies and feelings onto people wearing dog collars, thinking of them as better or worse than they really are, and the first lesson to learn as a curate is that the Vicar can all too easily turn out to be everyone's hated father, and the curate everyone's favourite brother. Now we have women priests of course, the images may be different but the dynamics could turn out to be the same.

Ele Hall, a kindly man who was aware of his own limitations, was quite happy to gather a team around him who would shine. This included Michael Langford, finishing off his doctorate, who went off to be Professor of Philosophy at St John's University, Newfoundland. Michael was a sharp and articulate apologist for a Christianity that was at once orthodox in its essentials, but liberal in the way it responded to modern findings and questions. He liked to excel in everything he took up. The other member was Joseph McCulloch, who was Rector of St Mary le Bow in the City. Bombed in the war, he had it rebuilt with two pulpits. This was a deliberately symbolic move, as he believed passionately that the church had to be in dialogue with the modern world, not just preach to it. It was here that he pioneered his dialogues with the more thoughtful celebrities of the age. The Bishop of London at the time, Robert Stopford, said in his dry way about Joseph, "Our one link with the outside world."

Because St Mary le Bow did not have services on a Sunday, he preached at St John's and many came to hear him. We also had a Cathedral standard choir at the time under Martindale Sidwell, and many other people came to hear the music. Sometimes if the Anthem at the 11 am Mattins was a long one it left Joseph only a short time for the sermon. On one Sunday Joseph got into the pulpit, made the sign of the cross and said, "Because we have had Buggins in H this morning, I can only speak for one minute," which he did and then climbed out of the pulpit. Joseph in his preaching showed how a sermon could be both interesting and important. People really did want to hear what he said. They thought he would cast some light on their lives. He was at his best for the Three Hour Meditation on Good Friday where he had time and could take a wide starting theme such as "the seven ages of man" before linking them into the words on the cross.

There was a paradox about Joseph. At the Three Hour service or celebrating the 12.15 Holy Communion which he did every Sunday with great devotion, something sublime could come through. Yet he could come across as one of the most egoistical of men, holding forth to an admiring circle with a cigarette in one hand in a long holder, and a glass of whisky in the other. The point about Joseph, however, was that he was deeply serious about the truth of the Christian faith and how best to communicate it in what he rightly saw to be a highly sceptical culture. He had the kind of seriousness about his vocation that we see reflected in the artistic integrity of great artists. His inspirations were above all William Blake and Carl Jung, and this led him to think in terms of the contrast between the "clamant ego" and our true self. It was that seriousness that so many clergy could learn from, as did I.[7]

Amongst Joseph's circle of friends were the novelists Ernest and Diana Raymond. Ernest, a former priest who had lost his faith in World War I and written a bestseller at the time, started to receive Holy Communion again during my time in Hampstead. Through him I met R.C. Hutchinson, one of the great overlooked novelists of the twentieth century, whom my brother, Charles, also discovered independently of me. Some of his novels, such as *A Child Possessed* and *Johanna at Daybreak* will one day be rediscovered.

I followed the familiar parish round, teaching some R.E. in our church school and finding myself not very good at it; taking Sunday School for the girls in the school for daughters of soldiers, visiting old people and newcomers, running youth clubs and so on. Some embarrassing memories of pastoral insensitivities on occasions come to mind. Also, some remarkable pastoral encounters. At the rather stately and old fashioned Mattins of those days a single man used to turn up. He told me his story. His parents had been drug addicts and his earliest memories were of them crawling round the floor. He came to this country and worked as a male prostitute. When he had finished telling me he burst out, "Out of this mess has come me!" Sadly, but understandably, as he was dying later in life he became bitter towards the church for its attitude to gay people and thought that I had not been active enough in opposing the church's attitude.

In Hampstead and later in Fulham we had our fair share of callers at the door. My wife and I still remember the perfectly charming Old Etonian as a result of whose visit our one bottle of champagne, carefully saved for our son's christening party, was emptied. Another was the man who told his favourite story of asking if the priest or minister believed God would provide. When the Vicar answered "Yes" he was told, "I know what, you give me what you have got for God is much more likely to provide for you than for me."

The period 1963–9 was an extraordinary one. As *Annus Mirabilis* by Philip Larkin put it, the miracle occurred in 1963 when sexual intercourse began which, he said, was rather late for him. It was not just the time of the Beatles and Lady Chatterley but of the Rolling Stones, drugs and Carnaby Street. Indeed, it is said that anyone who remembers the 1960s wasn't there, because if they had been they would have been stoned. Post-war austerity, discipline and restraint were thrown off in wild exuberance. The pill was approved for use in 1960, but even so, as I remember, there was the occasional sadness of an abortion by a young person.

Life with the young people of Hampstead at such a time was very stimulating. During school holidays I ran a series of discussion groups for older teenagers called "Out of doubt" in which we discussed the big issues of faith. I was also asked to chair "Arrowline", a secular organisation of more than a hundred local young people who used to meet together on Sunday evenings for socialising but who were also committed to service of the local community in various ways. This brings out a feature of the 1960s that is not often remarked on, and that is the idealism that went along with the desire to have a thoroughly good time. This was reflected in organisations like VSO, which enabled young people to serve overseas for a year, but at the political level in the defeat of the Conservative MP in Hampstead and the election of a Labour one, Ben Whitaker, with a Labour government under Harold Wilson in Parliament.

After three years in Hampstead I might have moved on but we were very happy and settled there and I was asked to combine being a curate with being Chaplain of Westfield College, just up the road. Founded as one of the first colleges for women in the University of London with a fine campus and a distinguished record it has sadly lost its identity in the series of mergers that have taken place in the University in recent decades. My time at Westfield was not a great success. First, the Principal was not popular, and I had to wake up to the fact that I was seen as someone who had been put in by him. But I did not really suit him either, as I wanted to introduce some more modern prayers at the daily morning worship but he and those who attended regularly just wanted the prayer book. Nor did my ministry suit the students, for they were all organised in tight little denominational groups, Anglicans being linked to the central chaplaincy in Bloomsbury, and they did not really want to do things together at Westfield or support the chapel there. I tried to get some serious outreach meetings going but not with any great success. I felt most at home with the younger members of staff.

Towards the end of the 1960s left-wing politics became more militant. In 1968 the Professor of Maths at Westfield went off to man the barricades in Paris. One evening I saw a young flame haired Paul Johnson (in recent years a right-wing commentator) striding across our school playground to speak at a meeting in our church hall in favour of the cultural revolution in China. In Christian circles it was a time of Christian Marxist dialogue. At Westfield I organised a number of meetings on this theme with dialogue partners such as Father Laurence Bright, a former nuclear physicist who became a Dominican monk and Marxist, and James Klugman, the saintly editor of *Marxism Today*. When I tackled him on the issue of needing to change individuals before society could really change, Klugman suggested that individuals begin to change as they try to change society. As part of this attempt to relate to people in the culture of the time, I showed Pasolini's film *The Gospel According to Matthew* at the Westfield arts festival. This, the only good film about Jesus in recent years, made by a Marxist, depicts a Jesus of great urgency and emotional power.

On 30 July 1966, Mark, our son was born. It was the day England won the world cup. During her pregnancy Jo had been in fine form as she continued her house job at the Whittington. But a few days after the birth something had clearly gone in her mind and she thought she had given birth to a son of God. Many years later we were able to laugh about it and say that in the light of the way Mark had turned out perhaps she was right! But at the time it was devastating. She was hospitalised for months. Luckily Mark went with her and the disturbance in the mind did not seem to affect the emotional bonding which is so crucial at that stage. Jo could not have been better looked after by a series of skilled consultant psychiatrists, but they were very puzzled by her case. At first, they diagnosed psychotic manic-depression as it was called in those days and then they veered towards a hysterical mimicking of this. But eventually after much treatment, including ECT she returned home. For Clare's birth we thought it would be safer to have the delivery at home, which we did and all went very quickly and safely, with her being born on 14 January 1969. Mark took one look at her after the birth and remarked, "Mummy, can we put it in the dustbin?" We were much helped at home by Miss Doddington, an elderly lady from a nearby block of flats who had spent all her life as a nanny. One of the great blessings of Hampstead was the many friends we made at the time, especially Bill and Christine Risbero and Piers and Poh Sim Plowright. Sadly, Piers, the distinguished BBC producer, died in 2021.

Pleasant though life was in Hampstead I could not stay there forever. I was surrounded on the whole by cultivated and liberal minded people. It is so easy to take up the attitudes of one's cultural environment and assume that all the world is like this. So it was important to move on. For the one time in my life I knew what I wanted to do, which was to become the vicar of a parish in London that was neither eclectic in its congregation or which worshipped what E.M. Forster called the great suburban Jehovah. But nothing seemed available. My area Bishop, Graham Leonard, the Bishop of Willesden, who led opposition to the ordination of women in the Church of England and who ended up a Roman Catholic, tried to palm me off with a totally unsuitable church. All seemed lined up for me to become the Vicar of Christ Church, Hampstead, and then the churchwardens there got cold feet about taking a curate from next door. I even looked at the possibility of school teaching for a bit. The Good Lord delivered me from all these possibilities when an advertisement appeared for someone to lecture in doctrine and ethics at Wells Theological College. I applied and was appointed. Three years later I received a letter from the Bishop of London, saying he remembered what I had been looking for and asked me to consider being Vicar of All Saints, Fulham, which was indeed exactly the kind of socially mixed, middle city parish with potential that I had been looking for. But in between we moved to Wells in Somerset. That same Bishop used to describe certain parishes as "a very stony part of the Lord's vineyard". Hampstead was a very pleasant part of that vineyard. My lot had indeed fallen onto goodly ground, as the psalmist put it.

Chapter 12

A good foundation

1969–1972

So, Jo and I and two small children found ourselves in a comfortable modern house tucked in just behind Vicar's Close in Wells, the oldest continuously inhabited street in Europe, looking out over the wonderful cathedral. It was a privilege to worship every day in the circular undercroft of the Cathedral and in the nave on Sundays, and to be surrounded by lovely countryside.

Shortly before I arrived Tom Baker, the Principal, had taken his staff across to the continent to experience the remarkable Christian community at Taizé as well as some of the best Roman Catholic worship as it had been renewed in the light of the Liturgical Movement, which had been gathering pace over the previous decade. The result was that the worship in the college was changed from a rather heavy Anglo-Catholicism to something lighter (but not shallow) and more participatory in its music, words and choreography. The other recent innovation had been to make small groups fundamental to the life of the college. Pioneered by Harold Wilson, the Principal of Salisbury theological college, all students had to be part of a small group which contained one staff member on an equal basis with the students. The group would meet at least once a week to discuss its life together and share at a reasonably deep level. In addition once a year a whole week was spent in T groups designed to bring about greater self-knowledge in the participants. I discovered then, as I confirmed later in parish life, that getting people to be a member of a small group in which there can be serious sharing deepens both the individual's faith and the life of the church in the way that is not possible just through membership of a large Sunday congregation.

In addition to Tom Baker, the staff consisted of Tony Barnard, who later went to be a Canon of Lichfield, David Mealand, who went to lecture in New Testament at Glasgow University and Keith Walker, an ex-Methodist historian who went on to Chichester and Winchester Cathedrals and did a great deal to pioneer the placing of modern works of art in churches. Tony Barnard, David Mealand and Tom Baker himself, who was a New Testament Scholar, had all been much influenced by Bultmann and the de-mythologizing school of Christianity. At Cambridge and Cuddesdon my work had been closely bound up with a study of the language and the texts and I had not been challenged by this radical school of interpretation, so the intellectual atmosphere was a salutary, bracing one. But for reasons described in my chapter on Cambridge I was convinced that the Christian faith, though containing mythological elements, was committed to certain factual assertions. When, for example, we put on a one day's conference on the Resurrection, I was the member of staff who, as a result of the influence of Donald Mackinnon, argued in favour of a real event which was both within as well as transcending history.

I had to deliver one solid lecture a week, one year on Doctrine I, God, Christ and Man, and the next year in Ethics. I was glad to teach Doctrine I, which seemed to me to raise the big questions for our time, rather than Doctrine II, Church, Ministry and Sacraments and anyway there were plenty of people working in that area to whom I felt the work could be safely left. These lectures required a great deal of preparation when given for the first time. In addition I had to conduct tutorials in the same subjects. The students were on the whole older than my generation at Cuddesdon, having done something else first. They needed guided reading and selected questions to address.

There is no doubt, however, that for me this solid teaching load laid an intellectual foundation which was indispensable for my work in subsequent years, for it is only when you begin to teach that you begin to realise how much you have to learn. I also began doctoral research on the principles of discrimination and proportion in the Just War tradition under Gordon Dunstan at King's College, London, which again was fundamental to my later work in the ethics of nuclear deterrence.

The 1960s were a lively time for public theological debate. After the furore over *Honest to God* and other even more radical theologies, *Time* magazine had a 1966 cover with the headline "God is Dead", with an article on the new Christian and Jewish theologians for whom, paradoxically, that seemed to be the starting point for a new theology. Then in 1969 *Time* magazine again ran a cover with a theological headline, this time with the words "God is alive again". In my lectures at the college covering this period I was an advocate of the German theologians Jürgen Moltmann and Wolfhart Pannenberg whose work gave rise to the second cover. Both these theologians had the future as a fundamental category of their thought, the former with a strong political cutting edge.

The teaching of ethics in the Church of England, always weak, had become almost non-existent. When I was at Cuddesdon we had a saintly parish priest, who had a first in law, to teach us some old-fashioned moral theology but it seemed to have no relation to modern issues. Wells was better than most colleges for my predecessor, Reggie Askew, who later followed me as Dean of King's College, London, had taught it with great enthusiasm, based on various case studies. He was also an enthusiast for the seventeenth-century Anglican Divines and we were fortunate in having an excellent library of their works at Wells which I could use for some of my research. Because the teaching of Ethics was in such a poor state, Sydney Evans, then Dean of King's, London, gathered a small team together to write a new syllabus and a handbook for teaching it. Sensibly he got us to stay in the shooting lodge of the Elphinstone estate in Scotland, at Glenmazeran, where we were locked away for a week with no possibility of accepting other engagements and the only distraction was going out to watch the eagles on our afternoon walk. The group included the philosopher Keith Ward, a lifelong friend, who served a title at Hampstead as a Non Stipendiary Minister whilst lecturing at Kings College, London, Ronald Preston of Manchester University, the only Christian ethicist who knew anything about economics and the learned and judicious Gordon Dunstan, also of Kings. Each of us wrote a different section. It was a seminal group and a formative week for me.[8]

It was during this time, in preparing my Ethics lectures at Wells that I came under the influence of the American thinker Reinhold Niebuhr. At Cambridge I had not been drawn to read his major theological tomes but going up to London in the train one day, I started to read his *Moral Man and Immoral Society*, which he later wished he had called "Immoral man and even more immoral society". It was a book that had originally been turned down by SCM in the 1930s as not a Christian book. It was a book about power in all its forms but especially economic and political power, and how power can best be contained in order to achieve some kind of justice in a world of self-interested groups. As I read the book it was as though a series of hammer blows were going on in my mind as his insights began to make sense of so much human struggle.

Niebuhr had been a key influence on leading Democrat politicians and academics from Jimmy Carter, who called his writings his political Bible, to Barack Obama, who was a huge admirer. His strength was not in his pure theology but in its application to the brutal world of politics, particularly international politics. His writings were to make me a realist, but always a hopeful one.[9]

It was a time of declining numbers of ordinands in the Church of England and small colleges like Wells were no longer financially viable, so Wells was merged with Salisbury. It was decided, for reasons that all later turned out to be false, to base the new college in Salisbury, rather than Wells. Wells staff moved there or elsewhere, but I stayed on as the first and last Warden of Wells, in order to see our final year students through to ordination.

The family were well settled. Mark was showing signs of great ability with his Cuisenaire rods at pre-school and Clare was blossoming. We were glad to be friends with Tony and Annie Barnard, who had a gift for friendship, other members of staff and people locally. We were very much bound up with life in the college but I did have one other creative endeavour locally. One Good Friday I hired a local mediaeval tithe barn together with a sound and light expert. I printed copies of the words of "Jesus Christ Superstar" and advertised the event in all the local newspapers. A very good crowd turned up to listen to the record being played and watch the lights revolve whilst if people wanted, they could follow the words on the script.

During this time Jo and I found the friendship of the artist Philippa Threlfall and her husband, Kennedy, who together ran the Black Dog pottery and produced some beautiful work, particularly supportive. Then as mentioned earlier, a letter arrived from Robert Stopford, the Bishop of London, remembering the kind of parish I was seeking and asking me to consider going to All Saints, Fulham. I had only been at Wells three years, but short as it was, my time there was crucial for so much which followed. Although my time as a student at Cuddesdon had been formative of the essentials of prayer and worship, Wells was much more adapted to facing the challenges of ministry in the modern world. It was also in tune with the best liturgical developments and in touch with the most challenging scholarship. Both Cuddesdon and Wells were committed to creating community but Wells, with its small group multicellular structure was able to do this at a deeper level. Above all the weekly discipline of research and teaching on fundamental doctrines and Christian Ethics provided a broad foundation on which I was able to build in subsequent years.

Chapter 13

Hard but rewarding

1972–1981

So I had found the mixed parish I was looking for. Fulham was an interesting area sociologically. Originally a series of market gardens supplying vegetables for London, it had been built up at the end of the nineteenth century to provide housing for senior clerks in the City who kept one servant. Then between the wars it went down market and parts became predominantly working class. The 1960s brought an advent of professionals with young children. All Saints, the old Fulham Parish Church, situated just to the North of Putney Bridge on the edge of Bishop's Park, was a handsome church. It was neighbour to Fulham Palace, at that time the oldest continuously inhabitant tenure of land in the country, having been in the hands of the Bishop of London since the seventh century. Until the Second World War it was the Bishop of London's country house, his town house being in Piccadilly! During the war cows were pastured in the grounds. The Vicarage was a well-built house with a sizeable garden between Fulham High Street, the Palace and the church.

All Saints was a somewhat quarrelsome parish in those days. There were three main groups, all totally dedicated to the church, but with a different vision of what this really involved. The previous vicar but one, who had had a long incumbency, was a high church bachelor terrified of women, who had instilled deep habits of worship and devotion into one group. They cared that worship was done well, that the church was properly looked after and that the festivals were kept with due joy and solemnity. Another group were primarily committed to serving the wider community and supported the boy scouts and other organisations. The third group, the social club, mainly of older people, maintained a busy programme of events, some of real distinction such as a recital in the church by pianist Moura Lympany. I remember going into the vestry before her recital to see that all was okay for her and found her on her knees praying. There was also an active and flourishing drama group.

I found that if I supported all the groups, which I wanted to do, and did not align myself too closely with anyone, then this rivalry could be kept in bounds. I saw that if each of the three groups had a dedication to the church that would put many smarter congregations to shame. Furthermore, I could see that at least in the case of one or two of the most difficult people they had a creative talent that had not been able to flower in their secular jobs because of their educational or social background. I remember some years later talking to a so called "coloured" priest in Apartheid South Africa and him telling me how difficult his PCC was. He told me that he was not too thrown by this because, as he put it, they were people who were constantly humiliated and rebuffed in their everyday lives and some of their frustration vented itself at church meetings.

The differences of opinion at Fulham came to a head in PCC meetings, and when I arrived in the parish they used to continue to midnight! I quickly put a stop to that with a finish by 10 pm at the very latest, on the grounds that you cannot make good decisions when you are tired. I also discovered within myself a certain low cunning which showed in the way I planned the agenda. I found that if there was a potentially divisive issue about which I cared strongly, such as introducing a new liturgy, the trick was to put it on the agenda immediately after a divisive one on which I had no strong views, for example, the church hall loos. People worked out their emotions on that and then the following item followed much more smoothly.

In his Pastoralia lectures at Cuddesdon, Bob Runcie had told us about the value of sometimes just "loitering with intent" in the parish. I was doing that one day in Hestercombe Avenue when I saw some people just moving in and introduced myself. It was David and Natasha Wilson who have been wonderful supportive friends since then. David agreed to come on the PCC and as I teased him when he later went off to be governor of Hong Kong, it would all be a doddle after the All Saints PCC.

My predecessor at All Saints had been on his last appointment before retirement, and was perhaps a slightly disappointed man. He also had a sharp manner which did not endear himself to people. But from my point of view he had done a valuable job in starting to bring about some changes in the liturgy which were necessary, although this had not made him popular. So, as a young man with a young family, I benefited from the reaction to him and experienced a wave of goodwill towards me. The rise and fall of congregational numbers always needs to be put in perspective. When some research on growing congregations was done once it was found that irrespective of churchmanship the main feature that growing congregations had in common was that the previous vicar had been there a long time!

The main service at All Saints was a dignified Sung Eucharist. I decided in addition to this to start a 35-minute, fast moving non-Eucharistic family service. This used drama, slides, modern music and involved participation. It also had periods of significant silence and prayer. It met a real need amongst the families with young children and quickly built up to a 100 or so. The difficulty that emerged was how to help members of this congregation come to appreciate and share the more stately Eucharist. I was interested to go back to All Saints many years later when under the wonderful Joe Hawes he had not only made the family service an abbreviated Eucharist, he had built up the numbers to several hundred.

The flourishing of All Saints in my time depended very significantly on the curates I was blessed to have as colleagues. First, Peter Kaye with his long black hair beautifully wavy and glossy. With his guitar and fine singing voice he introduced some good modern music into the family service. Then Chris

Moody and Peter Wheatley, both with me together for some of the time, intelligent, sensitive and musical. What a privilege it was to learn from them and have them as valued friends. Peter and Chris sang wonderful requiem masses together, which I have always wanted for myself. Peter was more definitely Catholic than I am. There was one particularly moving moment when after his first mass he invited his mother up the aisle to present her with a gift of flowers. However, I also remember being very surprised and shocked when he first told me he was opposed to the ordination of women. I was also joined by David Tann, a thoughtful priest who taught R.E. but who worked in the parish on a non-stipendiary basis, and Stephen Wilson who served his curacy at All Saints at the same time as conducting an intense engagement with a vibrant Hungarian girl he had recently met on a train and later married.

Parish work involved all the usual activities. In addition I found myself a trustee of umpteen small charitable trusts in the wider community. An advantage of this was that I met and worked on these with local councillors from the Fulham Labour party of olden days. The MP was Michael Stewart. These were good down to earth local people working hard for the community, as often as not with a cigarette in their mouths. I was chair of two sets of alms-houses and with the help of some of these councillors we managed to turn them into housing associations and obtain the money to make a difference. The Lygon Almshouses were pulled down and rebuilt as 40 modern warden assisted flats and the Sir William Powell ones, picturesque cottages next to the church, were extensively modernised.

The new Lygon building was opened by the Queen Mother and after the ceremony I showed her round. I took her into one flat where the resident lady got up from her seat, came close to the Queen Mother and gazing into her face said, "Oh, you are beautiful, you are beautiful." The nearest thing to spontaneous worship I had ever seen.

The influence of my time at Wells was seen in a number of ways. I encouraged as many people as possible to be a member of a small group, sometimes studying a book and sometimes the Bible. I also took a group of 30 or more away for a parish weekend once a year. I found that such weekends did more for parish life than a whole year of Sunday church going. Some innovations in the Liturgy also came from Wells, especially the Easter Vigil. Beginning with the Easter fire outside the church and then moving through the darkened church carrying the Paschal Candle for three stations of "Christ our Light", it comes to an early climax in the spine-tingling Exultet. It includes the vigil readings, long silences, baptisms and the Easter shout – ending with the Eucharist about midnight. Properly done it is the most thrilling service in the church's year and has a special power if Lent and the Triduum are kept properly. The only thing we did not have were the fireworks which are let off outside the church after such services in Greece.

Most Liturgical changes, however, came with the experimental services being published by the Church of England. The 1970s were a very creative time as far as parish liturgy was concerned and the parish was sympathetic to these innovations.

Music at All Saints then, however, was something of a problem as the organist found it difficult to build up a choir, so the standard was not high. I have always got on well with church organists because I make it quite clear I know nothing about music and am happy to leave it all to them. The problems begin if the vicar knows a lot about music, or worse, thinks he does, and has different ideas from the professional appointed for the job. However, I did want to raise the standard, and a group of highly talented musicians from the area formed themselves into a voluntary choir to sing once a month. Perhaps inevitably there were tensions with our regular choir master.

It was a very hopeful time as far as our relationship with Roman Catholics was concerned. The first documents of the

Anglican Roman Catholic Commission (ARCIC) were being published. This team of international scholars discovered that studying old problems by new methods had led to a remarkable convergence. On subjects like the Eucharist a huge amount of theology in common was identified and affirmed. Together with Adrian Hailer, priest of the nearby Roman Catholic church, we started a series of joint Anglican/Roman Catholic groups to the ARCIC documents. Later Adrian was to leave his ministry to get married. I had the pleasure of conducting a marriage service for him and Maggie in an Anglican church using a partly Roman Catholic liturgy. After retirement, we used to go for long walks together until his too early death.

I chaired two school governing bodies, our local primary school and St Mark's, a big Church of England Comprehensive, both catering for mainly working-class families with good jobs and sound values. St Mark's was not just an ex-grammar school with a Christian coating but a genuinely all ability school that took church seriously. Both schools gave me serious headaches with their heads.

As a parish priest, I experienced the familiar problem of lots of new families suddenly starting to come to church at the time when they required a letter from a Vicar saying they were a church member in order to get into a church school. Church schools were then and are now very popular with parents who value the discipline and values purveyed. Obviously having two schools locally benefited the church greatly and some of the parents of our primary school became very committed church members.

The head of St Mark's when I was there was a clever, tricky man who not only ran a good school but no less important always managed to outwit the London education authorities in their hostile policies towards church schools at the time. When he left under a cloud we had to appoint a new head. It was one of those occasions when I regretted not trusting my own judgement more. The main consensus of the governing body was for a very affable man whom we all liked, and I was alone in wanting a much tougher woman candidate. Wrongly, I went along with the general view rather than fighting it. A few years later, St Mark's was swept away in yet another educational reorganisation. This was a pity as it stood for something rather different, and I wonder what would have happened if I had trusted my own judgement more and been firmer in wanting the tougher woman candidate.

Clare went to a multi-ethnic, multiracial primary school in another part of Fulham, which she much enjoyed, before going on to Putney High School. Mark went to our own primary school. It was not easy for him coming into formed groups of working-class boys. More serious was the fact that the ultimate deterrent for the autocratic headmistress was to go and see "Vicar". Mark from having shown great promise was found bumping along on the bottom of the class. We got him some private tuition so he could pass the exam to Colet Court. After a year there, his work was so good he was offered a scholarship. A dramatic example, if one was needed, about the relationship between well-being and educational attainment. Living in the vicarage with us was a retired lady, Harriet Lloyd, who was glad to have somewhere comfortable to live. We were no less glad to have someone to help look after the children.

I went to All Saints, Fulham, at the age of 36, with some experience gained but still with energy and ambition to achieve something. Later, as Bishop of Oxford when I put priests of about that age into a new parish, I usually said that the ten years at this mid-period of one's life was, for that reason, usually crucial for those who want to make a real difference in their ministry. In retrospect I probably tried to do too many things on different fronts in the parish. There are also particular challenges in a parish about getting the work/life balance right. You live over the shop, as it were. You are only too ready to help if someone comes in genuine distress but when it is the church hall keys, you are not so motivated. I had no parish office or secretarial staff. It was always difficult to get a day off, though I made sure we had a good long holiday in the summer. Being a parish priest can be hugely rewarding as you have privileged access to people's lives at both high and low points. But it can also be a demanding one. I always used to say it was much easier being Bishop of Oxford than being Vicar of a growing parish. As Bishop of Oxford people had to get through the switchboard, then my secretary or chaplain, before they could get me on the phone. I had wonderful support staff and a prestigious position which protected me from the usual slights. As a parish priest you are at everyone's beck and call. There is also the cultural climate of today where there is so little wider validation of the vicar's role. The morale of many clergy is not high, and that has little to do with the stress of work but much do to with doubts about whether their life's work is valued by the society in which they live. If there are tensions in the congregation as well, this can be very sapping. I did not experience this but after nine demanding years of trying to develop the parish, it was probably right to move on.

As Vicar of All Saints Fulham at the opening of new housing for the elderly.

Chapter 14

The King of Deans

1981–7

I. The role

After nearly 9 years at All Saints, Fulham, I was not particularly looking for a new job, but first one person and then several more suggested that I apply for the position of Dean of King's College, London, which had recently been advertised. Eventually I did so because the new role for the Dean's job seemed to fit what I had to offer. Every Dean's job is different but the Deanship of King's is unique and very special.

King's College is an Anglican foundation. It was founded in reaction to University College, which allowed anyone who did not sign up for the Anglican establishment to obtain a degree, especially non-conformists but also non-believers. When King's was opened, an advertisement appeared saying that there was now no excuse for parents to send their offspring to the godless and infidel institution of Gower Street. King's then was a diarchy, with the Principal and Dean at the head. The Dean was responsible for the Theological Department and also the theological college, for the college was a major, indeed the largest, training establishment for Church of England ordinands. They lived in a large house in Vincent Square under the eagle eye of the Dean. There had been a number of highly revered Deans, especially in recent years Eric Abbott and Sydney Evans. Despite the political skills of the latter, he had lost two major battles. The theological department became a department of theology and religious studies with the Dean no longer its head, and the Church of England totally changed the training of ordinands, so they no longer did three years in Vincent Square under the eye of the Dean.

With my appointment the role for the Dean was rather different – to maintain the Anglican ethos of the college, supervise the chaplains and run the AKC course. This was a qualification unique to King's. Any student could sign up for a course of lectures in an aspect of basic theology, and if they passed the exam acquire the qualification "Associate of King's College" as well as their degree. In the early days it apparently brought an extra salary for teachers of £50 a year. 10 am on Mondays in the great hall was sacrosanct in the timetable for the AKC lecture. If students attended this regularly, which they had to in order to qualify, and passed an exam, which they could get through on the basis of lectures alone without extra reading, they could get this qualification. It was very popular, and several hundred students every year did the course. As the college expanded the lectures had to be delivered, either in person, or through recordings, on other sites as well. The Dean's job included organising this course, giving a lecture or two in it if the subject fitted his expertise, and getting the scripts examined and marked. At the same time he had to do a similar exercise for those reading theology, of whom still a high percentage intended to be ordained, in subjects other than theology, to widen their cultural grasps on such subjects as religion and literature, or classical civilisation. Again the Dean could give a lecture or two in this if it fitted.

The Dean, who was on the college council and who could be a trusted confidante of the Principal, was responsible for maintaining the Anglican ethos of the college. The Principal in my time was Neil Cameron, a devout Christian who had formerly been Chief of Defence. Sadly, he died in office. The Dean had overall responsibility for the chapel and team of chaplains, but they did the bulk of the actual pastoral work with students. He had a vast comfortable office in C corridor as it was then called, now turned into a student eating area, and two fulltime secretaries. So he was in a unique position of having some time and space in his life to do something creative. The college was interested in having me in post because of my profile on the airwaves and wanted me to do things outside the college, as well as within. Within the college it was important to keep good relationships with the various heads of departments because on them depended whether students were encouraged to do an AKC or not. In addition I was able to initiate a number of crossdisciplinary seminars with the academic staff on such subjects as "What is a university for?", and "Religion and literature."

King's is a great college, and I much appreciated its members of staff some of whom I got to know quite well. The bursar at the time was Myles Tempany, a daily mass going Catholic from the West coast of Ireland who served the college devotedly for the whole of his career and who was totally committed to its Anglican character. You never saw a piece of paper on his desk – all his business seemed to be done by warm human relationships across the college. Whenever I left his office after a visit, his farewell words were always "Keep the faith". His influence in the affairs of the college for its good was profound. During my time Myles recognised that a particular lecturer in the philosophy of religion had special abilities and manoeuvred first to get him made vice principal, and then, even though someone else had already been approached to take up the Principal's job, did more footwork to get him made Principal of the college. This philosopher of religion was Stewart Sutherland who went on to become Vice Chancellor of the University of London, Head of OFSTED, Principal and Vice Chancellor of Edinburgh University, a member of the House of Lords and generally one of the great and good in Scotland. All thoroughly deserved. I always much admired the way Stewart chaired Council meetings. He could outwit anyone there, but always with the genuine good of the college at heart. This combination of canniness and goodwill do not always go together but they did in him. Sadly, he died too young, but not before chairing the influential commission in Scotland on social care.

II. Nuclear Weapons

Both within and outside the college I was heavily involved in the debate on nuclear weapons. King's had a large and prestigious war studies department, and the college was situated near various important think tanks. I found myself Vice Chairman of the Council for Arms Control, which was set up to pursue multilateral as opposed to unilateral disarmament of nuclear weapons. I was also a member of the Pembroke Group and Chair of Shalom, all concerned with the ethics of force in one way or another. Later I became President of the Council on Christian Approaches to Defence and Disarmament (CCADD).

When I was on the staff of Wells Theological College, as mentioned earlier, I had started a doctorate on the principles of discrimination and proportion in the Just War tradition under Professor Gordon Dunstan of King's. A combination of the pressures of parish life, and a growing role in the media eventually led me to drop this, but not before I had done a great deal of work on the subject, which one way or another has found its way into print.

In 1982 my chapter "The morality of nuclear deterrence" appeared in *What hope in an armed world?*[10] which included contributions by Lawrence Freedman the distinguished head of the war studies department as well as Maurice Wilkins, the Nobel prize winner, who took a rather different view. Neil Cameron, the Principal, was the one who initiated this book and asked me to contribute. He was an interesting man who had left school at 16 with no qualifications and joined the RAF. Despite having crashed a plane and being demoted as a result in the early stages of his career, he had risen to be head of the RAF and then Chief of the Defence staff. A handsome man, of tough charm, who could not string two sentences together in writing, he communicated powerfully mainly through his body language. He rightly saw that in the world of London University politics if you were not getting bigger you were likely to be swallowed up by others, so in his time King's took in both Chelsea and Queen Elizabeth Colleges, and resisted a merger with Bedford College. He once remarked that the fighting between service chiefs for defence resources was nothing compared to the in-fighting of university politics in London.

When Neil Cameron asked me to contribute to the book, it was obvious that I was expected to offer some kind of defence for a policy of nuclear deterrence. In fact I was rather uncertain at the time. Could nuclear weapons ever be used in a way that was both discriminate and proportionate? And what was the morality of threatening to use them if they could never be used in such a way? Though at that point uncertain about the answer to that question, I did believe that the nuclear standoff was fundamentally stable, that there was a nuclear stalemate, and that for the first time in the history of the world it could never be in the interest of one power to use nuclear weapons against another. That of course makes two assumptions, that the powers will always act rationally, and that there are no accidents. Anyway with moral trembling and spiritual fear, which should always belong to the justification of force, I did contribute to the book.

This leads on to the biggest intellectual influence on my life during this period, Michael Quinlan. Michael, a very senior civil servant who was both the architect of British nuclear policy and a devout Roman Catholic sought to develop this policy in accord with the principles of discrimination and proportion from the Just War tradition. He had one of the best analytical brains I know, and when I suggested this might have been developed in his time as a civil servant, he attributed it instead to his Jesuit schooling. He was greatly respected by all who knew him in the Civil Service and in Government and hugely influential in the circles in which I moved, that is those trying to think through the morality of nuclear weapons. The results of my academic research, the influence of Michael and the many discussions I was having at this time came together in my book *Christianity and War in a Nuclear Age*.[11] This defence of Nuclear Deterrence resulted in a hostile story in the Guardian when I went to Oxford, which meant I aroused suspicion amongst peace campaigners. Later, with the world in a very different place, I became critical of the drive to replace Trident.[12] It also seems absurd for the British government to increase the number of nuclear warheads, as it did in 2021. No doubt there is still a case for retaining a minimum deterrent with Russia under Putin putting such pressure on its neighbour, but I have long argued that the greatest threat in the modern world is in fact cyber warfare, and it is pointless relying on nuclear weapons if a country's whole command and control system can be disabled.

The public debate on nuclear weapons was very much alive in the 1980s and I often found myself on public platforms opposing people like Bruce Kent and Paul Oestreicher. Bruce Kent I found difficult to engage with, as he tended to make ad hominem points. But Paul was a serious opponent on this issue and we had some important, respectful arguments.

At Fulham I had attended a long mid-service clergy course at St George's, Windsor. As my thesis for this I did work on the Christian attitude to revolutionary violence. This was another key issue at the time because of liberation movements in South Africa and liberation theology in South America. The debate was divided between those who were uncritically supporting these movements or, more usually, uncritically condemning all use of force in overthrowing unjust regimes. I wanted to show that there was a tradition of Christian thinking on this akin to the Just War criteria and eventually this took the form of a short book. My position then and now is that you cannot jump straight from a theological position to a political programme.

First the theology has to be spelt out in the form of ethical considerations and then these in turn have to be applied in relation to a particular political situation after that has been properly analysed. I argued that there can be such a thing as a just revolution, but only if certain criteria are met and each struggle has to be considered in this light. The bare fact of a manifestly unjust regime is not enough to justify an attempt at a violent overthrow.

I was disappointed that in the end the book was published without my footnotes and that it received so little attention, when in fact it might have brought some clarity to a contentious debate.[13]

III. South Africa

In 1982 I was invited to give some lectures at St Mary's Cathedral, Johannesburg, and this became a transformative experience.[14] The trip began in an interesting way with me being refused entry at the airport. They claimed that these lectures were work and I did not have a work permit. The people meeting me had to ring up the leader of the opposition in parliament, Frederik van Zyl Slabbert, who was on the golf course at the time. He managed to persuade the authorities to let me in. That night there was a party to welcome me and when I told Desmond Tutu about this incident he literally rolled round and round the veranda, laughing his head off and saying, "They would not let the Dean of King's in." Desmond had done his degree at Kings and was a huge admirer of the college, saying he was prouder of being a Fellow of King's than any of his other honorary awards and degrees. I spent a wonderful evening with him in his house in Soweto, with him sipping rum and Coca Cola and breaking into laughter as we watched a satirical film on TV about the second coming with Desmond himself being portrayed as that coming figure. It has been such a privilege to know a man of such deep spirituality and personal bravery, with his willingness to speak the truth to power be they black or white; always indomitable in the pursuit of justice but always with a view to turning enemies into friends, and of course, that captivating humour, smile and laughter.

Whilst in South Africa I had the opportunity to meet other the key leaders, including Beyers Naudé, who was under house arrest, and who hugely impressed me by his moral strength and integrity. He was a key figure in eventually getting the Dutch Reformed Church to repent of its support of Apartheid. I also met Archbishop Dennis Hurley the Roman Catholic Archbishop in Natal. On the way there I was able to call in and meet Anthony and Maggie Barker, both doctors, who spent their whole life running the hospital in Nqutu performing every kind of operation.[15] When they later returned to work in England, I had the opportunity to meet up with them again, two of the most selfless people I have ever met. Sadly they were both killed by a truck whilst riding a tandem bicycle. I also went to Witwatersrand University to represent King's College, as an old student, Helen Joseph, was given an award for her resistance to apartheid. This provided an opportunity to have lunch with the great novelist Nadine Gordimer in her house. Her novel *July's people* was an important influence on me, in the way it reinforced my understanding of power and the deceptions of power. Above all I had the opportunity to experience the dignity, vitality and political integrity of some of the congregations in Soweto. They were truly life giving and inspiring. So too was the Cathedral, with its mixed race congregation. The telephonist at the Cathedral used to take services on Sundays in Johannesburg prison in five different languages! The Dean, Simeon Nkoane was a saintly man, a member of the Community of the Resurrection, whose best-known figure was Father Trevor Huddleston. Simeon was a gentle person of prayer but when he was made bishop of Johannesburg showed great courage going into crowds which were about to "necklace" some poor soul, to try to dissuade them.[16]

When I returned from South Africa, I wrote a couple of articles for *The Times* about my experience and as a result was asked by David Haslam to chair End Loans to South Africa (ELTSA) whose purpose was to do just that: stop banks lending the money which helped prop up the South African economy. Many forces helped to bring about the end of Apartheid but there is no doubt that the final refusal of the banks in New York to continue to lend to the South African government was a crucial factor. David Haslam is a great campaigner for a number of different causes and we need more people like him to push people like myself into action.

As well as the usual task of chairing board meetings I went with others to the AGMs of major financial institutions which were working in South Africa. In particular we all had one Barclay's share, so were able to go to that Bank's AGM and raise questions about their position in there. It was salutary to stand and start my question only to be hissed at from all around the floor. A minor indignity compared to the kind of cruelties being perpetuated under Apartheid of course.

When miraculously apartheid came to an end without significant bloodshed I, along with other campaigners, was invited along to the South African embassy in London to see the inauguration of Nelson Mandela on a large TV screen. It was one of the most moving moments of my life.

My visit to South Africa had other repercussions. Some members of the General Synod of the Church of England had for many years been campaigning to get the Church Commissioners to stop investing in companies which had business interests there. The Commissioners always argued that whilst they had reduced their stake in these companies, their fiduciary duty was to maximise financial returns in order to support the ministry of the church. Under the wily leadership of Sir Douglas Lovelock it proved virtually impossible for us to get a handle on this issue. Officially all the bishops are commissioners, but in fact they take no responsibility for investment decisions. These are made by the assets committee which seemed to be a law unto itself. Eventually, in frustration, Christians Concerned with South Africa (CCSA) decided the only way to really get the issue discussed was to take the Commissioners to court. Andrew Philips (later Lord Philips of Sudbury) provided the pro-bono service of his firm Bates, Wells, Braithwaite and a simple advertisement very quickly raised the £30,000 we needed to cover our costs in case we lost the case. By then I had become Bishop of Oxford, and I was put in as front man to fight the case. Our argument was that the purpose of the commissioners was above all to promote the gospel, of which paying the clergy was a means to that end. The Commissioners took a different view, and in the end the judge did not uphold our position. But along the way in his judgement, he made some highly significant points which not only clarified how far trustees are allowed to take ethical considerations into account in the affairs of a charity but significantly widened out most people's understanding of what was possible in the way of bringing ethical principles to bear. The case was a significant one and at least I will go down in history as a footnote in legal textbooks. People come up to me and say how important that judgement still is. We paid our own costs but did not have to bear the much larger costs of the commissioners.

Douglas Lovelock got the press on his side with hostile headlines to the effect that I was going to cost the church a large sum of money, so I was the recipient of some hostility. He also somehow persuaded a Liberal MP who should have known better to ask a question hostile to me in parliament. Some years later I was glad when that MP had the grace to apologise to me for this.

People have sometimes been perplexed about where I stood on the political spectrum. On the one hand I was at this time a robust defender of a policy of nuclear deterrence. On the other hand I supported liberation movements and actively campaigned against apartheid. For those who think in simple left and right terms this might appear a contradiction. But the consistency lies in how I view power. Ever since I had read Reinhold Niebuhr's *Moral Man and Immoral Society* I was convinced that the key moral question for society is how power can best be contained and tempered in the interests of justice. This means all power, economic as well as military.[17] This led me on the one hand to think that a rough and ready justice could only be secured in a world of warring superpowers by ensuring that it could never be in the interest of either of them to start a war. It also led me to think that economic power can and ought to be used to achieve as much justice as possible in the political sphere. In fact my position was not as unusual as it might appear but fitted easily into the traditional wing of the labour party as represented, for example, by that fine man Dennis Healey. Even when I was in my seventies, he always addressed me with the words, "Hello, young man, how are you?" When he retired, Dennis Healey used to sit with his wife in the evenings listening to music. From time to time one of them would slip a note to the other with just three letters on it, AWL. (Aren't we lucky.)

It is easy to talk about peace but what is needed is a just peace, which is what is meant by the Hebrew word Shalom. The prayer of the Corrymeela Community, dedicated to peace building in Northern Ireland sums up well how we should think and pray about it.

Show us, good Lord,
The peace we should seek,
The peace we must give,
The peace we can keep,
The peace we must forego,
And the peace you have given
In Jesus Christ our Lord.[18]

IV. The Soviet Union

My position at King's also gave me the opportunity and time to do some official travelling. One trip was as a member of a peace delegation to Moscow, Latvia and Georgia. Led by Paul Oestreicher, it was mainly composed of unilateralists, but Paul with his usual fairmindedness wanted to include me as someone prepared to defend a policy of nuclear deterrence. Moscow at the height of the cold war was an extraordinary place. We stayed in the Ukraine Hotel, one of Stalin's famous gothic skyscrapers in the heart of Moscow with its spacious but bare rooms, and an old woman on each floor keeping an eye on who came and went. There were tickets for the frugal meals, and once I nearly got into big trouble by going into one of the dining rooms and sitting down to a breakfast meant for another group. The meetings with officials were very formal, long platitudinous speeches all around. One such meeting was suddenly electrified when Donald Reeves, one of our group, suddenly thumped the table and to a group gently dozing after lunch, expressed his anger at the refusal of the Soviet Union to allow the son of Tarkovsky, the film maker to join his father outside the Soviet Union.

We were able to meet dissidents only in the street for fear of being bugged. One told us that his apartment had been raided when he was out and when he came back he was confronted by some KGB men who held up a medallion of the Pope, pointing to it and saying accusingly "CIA agent". When he explained that he was a member of an ecumenical prayer group and the medal had been given to him by one of the Roman Catholic members, the burly KGB man, steeped in State atheism as he was, drew himself up and said, "There is only one true church, the Orthodox Church."

We also met dignitaries of the Orthodox Church of course, including Metropolitan Philaret of Minsk and Byelorussia who later came to my consecration as Bishop of Oxford and presented me with a large pectoral cross. A large, bulky man with long dark sleeked back hair, I vividly remember him expatiating at length about how the Orthodox church always had been and continued to be a patriotic church, supporting government. During the peroration he had one hand pointing to the ceiling. It was clear this speech was not just for us but for those listening to the bugged recording. In fact, as Michael Bordeaux of Keston College revealed, when all the KGB files were opened, nearly every dignitary of the church was in one way or another in the hands of the KGB. But who are we to judge what was or was not possible at the time? Despite periods of very fierce persecution, the Orthodox Church somehow survived. First, because the faith was deeply embedded in the people. A story is told of an atheist propagandist giving a speech to assembled villagers in one of the periods of repression. When he had finished someone in the crowd simply shouted out "Christ is Risen", and the people replied with their ancient Easter response, "He is risen indeed." Secondly, this faith was particularly deeply imbued in the grandmothers, the babushkas, and it is they more than anyone who kept the faith alive. A good example is Mr Putin's mother, a Christian, whom Putin apparently reveres and after whose example, it is claimed, he is a believer. Thirdly, there is the story of one young priest. I asked him how he had come to faith and then been ordained at a time of religious repression. He said first of all it was the aesthetic and spiritual beauty of the icons and music of the church that had drawn him. Secondly, he said that in the books of atheist propaganda there were long quotations from Christian writers. It was through these that he learnt about the faith and was further drawn into it.

I have always found Russia a deeply moving place to visit, taking one close to tears. One reason for this is an awareness of the terrible losses which they suffered in World War II, over 20 million, which are remembered in their great memorials before which a flame burns. Then of course there is the suffering of the

Communist period. But it also has to do with the extremes of the Russian temperament, with its willingness to ask fundamental questions, always poised between ecstasy and despair, both of which are so apparent in the novels of Dostoevsky which have so influenced me. That Russian temperament seems a much more truthful, if less pragmatic, response to the reality of life than the average English person's phlegmatic indifference to big questions.

The quickness and humour of those we met always astonished us. Galina our interpreter, in her expensive French silk scarves, was quicker on the uptake on English jokes than we were. When not otherwise occupied the interpreters enjoyed playing Monopoly complete with the English names on the board, Mayfair, Regent Street etc. Perhaps my favourite joke, from the time when Communism was crumbling was the one which said the party was offering 50 roubles to anyone who renewed their membership. Then, if they managed to recruit someone else to join, not only would they get their 50 roubles they themselves could leave. Finally, if they recruited two new members not only would they be able to leave they would receive a certificate saying that they had never been members. Russian jokes, like Jewish ones were wrought out of suffering.

There were some wonderful paradoxes. In Moscow once we were shown into a classroom where they taught English. One wall was given over to images of Scottish tartans and clans. In large letters on thefront wall was written "My heart is in the highlands", a line of Robert Burns, who is revered in Russia as a peasant poet. In the same classroom I picked up a book on British history. One chapter was given to the Church of England. Its opening line was "The Church of England is a creation of the state which has never been popular with the people"!

Another paradox was the apparent opulence of the Orthodox Church. This expressed itself not only in the most lavish hospitality I have ever encountered but in the little packets of roubles which we were all given as spending money when we arrived. The reason for this wealth was that the state took all responsibility for the upkeep of such churches as they allowed to exist, as well as the salaries of the clergy. This meant that all the money from the sale of candles, a huge amount, I was told, was available for other things.

This peace delegation visited Latvia, Moscow and Georgia. That visit to Georgia was the first of a number I have paid to that wonderful country. Each visit seemed to be at a crucial stage in its history, and I have written about these later in this book.

My next visit to Moscow was to represent the Archbishop of Canterbury at a conference of religious world leaders on weapons in space. The Orthodox Church had an important role in Communist propaganda both in relating to the West and in putting a favourable gloss on the regime. This resulted in the church mounting big international conferences which would produce resolutions supporting the Communist line. The reason for this conference was that the Americans were rapidly developing ballistic missiles and satellites which could shoot down incoming nuclear weapons and so provide a shield. Being behind technologically in this field, and fearful of the unlimited expense of developing such weapons themselves, the Russian government wanted this development roundly condemned. In fact I had no problem doing just that, because I believed first that there could never be such a thing as a real shield from nuclear missiles, for if even only one weapon got through that would be enough to cause massive devastation. Secondly, because it made the whole deterrent system suddenly uncertain and therefore perhaps tempting for one side to try to get through such a shield with a surprise attack. The point about deterrence was the absolute certainty that it could not be in the interest of either side to fire a missile, and the prospect of a shield in space loosened that certainty.

When the cold war ended, I was involved in trying to bring about some practical co-operation between the Church of England and the Orthodox Church. At that time the Church in Russia had a golden opportunity not just to celebrate the liturgy but to try to contribute to wider society. There were various ways in which we could offer expertise in areas which were new for them, such as chaplaincies in prisons, hospitals and the services, and also in various forms of social care. Not a great deal came from these initiatives and one reason was the increasing coldness of the Orthodox Church towards the Church of England because of the move to ordain women. This came to a dramatic head later on a visit I paid with the Archbishop of Canterbury, George Carey, when at the last moment the visit was downgraded from an official visit to the church as a whole to a private visit of the Archbishop to the Patriarch. The hospitality immediately became less, and some of us were even forced to share rooms. The Russian church, like its government, has no scruples about exerting its power or letting others experience its displeasure.

V. Swan Hellenic

As a result of recommendations by the Professor of Greek and the Professor of Byzantine Studies at King's, I became a regular lecturer on Swan Hellenic cruises. These began after World War II and were associated with a big-name TV scholar, Sir Mortimer Wheeler. They combined high culture with hard living in an old Turkish Boat, the Ankara. Carrying passengers such as high powered civil servants who had got a first in Greats many years before, the lecturers were the top names in the field. But they had to live without many creature comforts. By the time I became a lecturer in the early 1980s, the ship was the Orpheus, originally on service from Britain to Northern Ireland but by then was staffed by an all-Greek Crew. The fellow lecturers still included people at the front line of scholarship like John Chadwick who with Michael Ventris cracked the Linear B script. I can still remember vividly some of the wonderful lectures and talks. Michael McClagan of Trinity College, Oxford, reduced the whole audience to tears with his lecture on the fourth crusade in 1204 and the fall of Constantinople in 1453. I can still picture John Luce, the Professor of Classics at Trinity College, Dublin, standing on the walls of Troy which have been built and rebuilt at least seven times over the millennia. I used his moving words he spoke then to end my book on nuclear weapons.

One of the five lecturers was a priest, hence my presence in this august gathering. For there was a Holy Communion on Sundays, always rather well attended. I used to say if you wonder where the Church of England is, it was on a Swan Hellenic cruise! For it was a particular kind of professional clientele who went on these cruises, the ship often carrying literally scores of doctors travelling anonymously. After Bob Runcie, a regular lecturer, started worrying about the fact that the passengers but not the crew had a service, we started taking a service in the crew quarters as well. By this time there was a larger boat, the Minerva I, staffed by a combination of Philippine men and women and Ukrainians. The Philippine crew were often devout Roman Catholics and they played simple religious refrains on their guitars. So we had the unusual experience of celebrating an Anglican liturgy, with an occasional reference to Mary, for a Roman Catholic congregation all willing to receive Holy Communion.

The cruise consisted of two-week hops, originally in the Mediterranean and then later with a bigger ship in the Far East and the Americas, with summer cruises to the Baltic and Norway. I used to lecture on the religion and culture of the areas we were going to visit, including its religious art. Sometimes because the management wanted a particular lecture or site talk, and we all had to do a set number, you found yourself well out of your comfort zone. Owen Chadwick used to lecture on these cruises but eventually stopped. When I asked him why he said, "Well, Richard, I began to feel so bogus." "Well Owen," I replied, "how do you think most of us feel most of the time." In fact the clergy/lecturers were on the whole good lecturers. The lecture needed to be informative but also accessible with a touch of humour and the clergy often succeeded in this better than some more specialised academics. I was fortunate in being able to go to many parts of the world on these cruises. I much enjoyed the process of research, building on some area I knew something about but enlarging it and then the lecturing itself and the company.[19] My wife and I made some life-long friends through these cruises. It was a huge bonus and enrichment to our lives. Sadly in 2016 Swan Hellenic went bankrupt.

A very able priest told me once that the only job in the Church of England he had ever coveted was to be Dean of King's. I certainly found it a wonderful position. I much enjoyed my contact with staff and students and my work in the college. And I much appreciated the fact that the college wanted me to play a role outside the college. One of those roles was in the media.

Chapter 15

The Media

In 1967 when I was in Hampstead there was a military coup in Greece in which four colonels took over the government. They did so in the name of Christianity. This so incensed me that I penned an article showing the incompatibility of what they stood for and the Christian faith and sent it off to *The Guardian*. Christopher Driver, the features editor, wrote back a nice letter to say that he much liked the article but was it written out of first-hand experience of Greece, and of course I had to say no. So I sent the article to *New Christian,* a lively new magazine funded by Timothy Beaumont and edited by Trevor Beeson. They published it and as a result asked me to do occasional reviews and writing for them. When in 1972 I came back to London from Wells, someone had clearly seen my writing and recommended my name to the BBC. They tried me out for some scripts for "Prayer for the Day", approved and kept me on.

Amongst the many major changes that have taken place in my lifetime are those which have happened in the BBC. In those days, when the aura of Lord Reith still hung over the BBC, the Head of Religious Broadcasting was a senior Anglican Clergyman who had direct access to the Director General. There was always a Roman Catholic priest on the staff, and it usually fell to him to produce "Prayer for the Day". In those days "Prayer for the Day" was the same as "Thought for the Day" except that it ended with literally a one-line prayer in which the thought was focussed. It was broadcast at 6.50 and though it had to be related to the news this was interpreted very widely and I could use a lot of poetry and literature. I found the audience very receptive. I used to pre-record several scripts in advance. Then, after a period I got bored of pre-recording and started to do them live. I did this all through the Falklands War, including the sinking of the Belgrano, so far as I know without a single complaint. Then according to David Winter, the Head of Religious Broadcasting at the time, he woke up in a sweat one night and realised I had been doing it live for several months without my scripts being checked by a producer.The difference now could not be more striking. The script, under the supervision of the Religion and Ethics Department, has to be signed off by both the producer of the day and the head of the department. Every word is weighed for balance and possible bias or misunderstanding. The person doing the broadcast might get a call in the middle of the night or when they arrive in the studio because of a worry about the script that had suddenly struck them. The BBC is so under attack and the slot is such an exposed one, being broadcast at peak listening time to an influential listenership, that the producers feel highly nervous about complaints. That said, I have found the producers of real help over the years. Their trained ears can spot when a sentence is not clear or misleading. I would like to pay tribute to them, especially Christine Morgan, the Head of Religion and Ethics for many years until she retired recently.

Another change is that in those days the producer's main concern was that you got the tone of the broadcast right. I remember one of my first producers, Roy Trevivian, saying to me in his warm regional accent, "Imagine that there is an old lady sitting in an arm chair. You have your arms round her and you are talking to her." That may or may not be the best way for all of us, but what E.M. Forster said about the novel, "Get the tone right and everything else follows", is certainly even more true of broadcasting than it is of writing.

I did "Prayer for the Day" every week for about eleven years without a break. Lionel Blue did Mondays and I did Fridays. Lionel was a unique broadcaster and no one could match his experience, which included the brothels of Amsterdam when he was young, or his humour. He came to All Saints, Fulham, to take part in an Evening Dialogue with me during Advent one year and admitted that every Christmas he teetered on the edge of Christianity so affected was he by the Christmas story and its atmosphere. Apart from any major influence on me there was one minor one. When I retired as Bishop of Oxford, Jo and I dined with him and his partner in North London. I shared with him the dilemma as to whether or not to wear a dog collar or a tie now I was retired. He was adamant that I should continue to wear a dog collar, which I always do in the Lords and at formal events, though not in the parish except when I am taking services.

Going into the studio to do my broadcast live meant that I got to know Brian Redhead and John Timpson, the presenters in those days. Brian Redhead's faith took on a new strength when one of his twin sons was tragically killed. He used to tell me about walks around the village with his much admired Vicar, an ex-miner who bred whippets. There was even a period when it was widely believed that Brian himself would seek ordination. When it came to the prayer at the end of my script, he would put his hands together and bow his head, at least half seriously, as he had been taught at School.[20]

When "Prayer for the Day" was taken out of the *Today* programme and made a self-contained religious slot before the programme itself started, I switched to "Thought for the Day". I still like to do Fridays but not so frequently, and at present I do three sets of three in a year, which is right for what I want to do now. It is not an easy slot to fill. First of all it has to be related to the news in some way. Secondly, it has to tease out a theological dimension, but to do so in a way that is accessible to a largely non-religious audience as they are going about their daily tasks. Thirdly, it must have something worthwhile to say that is not platitudinous or sound like a sermon.

I have three questions that I try to ask myself about a broadcast. First, is it interesting? E. M. Forster, as well as writing about the importance of getting the tone right, also wrote that the first requirement of the novelist is to get the reader to turn the page. This is a real challenge for any form of religious communication today as so many people switch off at the first hint of a religious theme, and this is, sadly, because many of them are so utterly predictable. As soon as a sentence is uttered people know what is going to follow. I certainly cannot claim that all my broadcasts are of universal interest, and of course people are interested in different things. But I can at least ask whether it interests me. If it bores me it will certainly bore everyone else, and it helps that I have a very low threshold of boredom. The great model for broadcasting here is Alastair Cook. In his "Letter from America" you could never quite tell where he was going until the end.

Secondly, is it true? There are all kinds of stories and statements that are fascinating but simply not true. Before anything else, Christians are in the truth business. So a talk must not only be interesting, what is said must be true. It is possible to exaggerate, overstate widely and slant the argument to win attention. But in the long run this undermines trust in what you say.

Thirdly, is it helpful? For it is possible to say things which are both interesting and truthful but not helpful for that particular audience at that particular time to hear. For a Christian communicator there is a further dimension and challenge. It is not just you that you want the audience to hear but you want the Holy Spirit to speak to them. "Deep calls to deep" as psalm 42 puts it, or in the words of Cardinal Newman's motto. *Cor ad cor loquitur,* heart speaks to heart. So the speaker's prayer must be that the Holy Spirt in their own heart might speak to the Holy Spirit in the heart of the hearer. And of course it must not be, or sound to be, pious.

It is not an easy slot to fill but it is a great privilege. The *Today* presenters at the time of writing, Justin Webb, Mishal Husain, Nick Robinson and Martha Kearney (and before them Sue MacGregor, Evan Davis, Ed Stourton, Jim Naughtie and Sarah Montagu) have always been very welcoming and friendly, which makes it easier. John Humphrys, who has recently retired, despite his public dislike of the slot has always been particularly friendly and it really counts when he has given me thumbs up after a broadcast.

Preaching is not easy. People who have given a sermon don't always realise how difficult it is, but if they are asked, as sometimes happens, they quickly discover how hard it is. It is easier to deliver a lecture in which something interesting and informative is required. But a sermon is expected to have a message and to offer both spiritual uplift and a moral challenge as well. Although people have sometimes said that they have found a particular sermon of mine helpful, I do not regard myself as a good preacher. I dislike theatricality in the pulpit and I find it false to deliberately try to stir people's emotions. The sermons I like to hear are short, deeply thought through and carefully crafted. I am happy to close my eyes and listen as it is read. "Prayer for the Day" and "Thought for the Day", however, provide a format that suits me well. They are short, only 2 minutes 45 seconds now. But that is no problem, as I admire Clement Attlee about whom it was said that he never used one word when none would do. A great deal can be said in that short time, and a carefully written "Thought" can easily be expanded into a ten-minute sermon that says nothing more. In fact with its tight limits of time and expectation it is best treated as a mini art form.

Sometimes it is not easy to see what there is in the news that lends itself to a theological treatment in a way that is not platitudinous, political or polemical. It is easier when there is some big subject that is inescapable, as I have experienced from time to time. Sometimes a script has to be torn up and a new start made because of some breaking news. And sometimes the news comes late. I was woken up early, told that Princess Diana had died and would I do "Thought". On that occasion and others when the news is major all the speaker has to do is to capture the mood of the nation and articulate it. The last thing needed on such occasions is anything clever, or even very original. Another tragic event was the Zeebrugge ferry disaster on 6 March 1987 when the Herald of Free Enterprise was sunk with 193 people drowned. I found that some words from Gerald Manley Hopkins's poem *The wreck of the Deutschland* came to my aid in the middle of the night to help me with my script. The BBC published a collection of my talks in 1975 and since then three other collections have been published by different publishers.[21]

I have done bits and pieces of other radio over the years and some television, and it has been a great privilege to have such opportunities. But a senior church figure is always in a bit of a bind when being interviewed about some contemporary, probably controversial, issue. The reporter wants some response that will make an impact, that is, it will be controversial. The Bishop will want to use the opportunity to get his or her message out but will want to do so without falling into traps laid by the questions. In our media training we were offered a simple ABC tip in how to handle this. A, acknowledge the question. B, bridge this to what you were saying and then C, continue.

As a result of my broadcasting I have been asked over the years to write for the newspapers, and at one time wrote reasonably regularly for *The Observer*. As a result of my broadcasting, publishers also became interested and I began to write books.[22] My books have never had big sales. I don't write for the popular evangelical market, where sales are high, and I have never been a cult figure. But there are, I know, at least some people on my wavelength, who want something thoughtful that faces the intellectual challenges of our time whilst being faithful to Christian orthodoxy. Like me there are people who recognise that poets and novelists can give depth and freshness to a Christian language that has for so many become either stale or meaningless.

With Jo about to go to Oxford in 1987.

Chapter 16

Oxford

I. Friends and colleagues

I was certainly not looking for a move from King's. The position of Dean could not have been a more wonderful one, a prestigious position within a friendly college and, almost uniquely, enough time to pursue a range of interests both within and outside the college. Furthermore as a family we were very well settled in Barnes in our own house, Mark and Clare having gone to school locally before going to university. Then an important looking envelope dropped through the letter box. It was from the Prime Minister, Mrs Thatcher, asking whether I would be willing for my name to go forward to the Queen to be the next Bishop of Oxford. I did not even know the diocese of Oxford was vacant. Neither Jo nor I was filled with immediate delight, so settled and happy were we in both job and home. We consoled ourselves by saying, "At least we will be living at Cuddesdon." For the Bishop's Palace, when I was at the theological college, was just across the road, and enjoyed wonderful views over the countryside. Nevertheless, it was of course a great honour to be offered such a position and there would have had to have been very good reasons to refuse such a responsibility.

Our hope of moving to Cuddesdon was quickly dispelled. My predecessor, Patrick Rogers, had, for various reasons, moved into Oxford, to 27 Linton Road, next door to Wolfson College. It was a substantial Edwardian house, whose great joy was the garden. The Queen Mother once asked me where my palace was. I told her I no longer lived in a palace but a house well described as being of "Edwardian amplitude". "Oh, how awful," she replied. I don't know quite what she thought I was living in. A previous occupant, a clergyman known as Cross of Jesus as opposed to Cross of Christ Church had a wife who was blind. A keen gardener, she had planted the garden to maximise the scents and she had the money to keep up the very large area. Allegedly in those days Bishops might sometimes put the initials WHM after the name of one of their clergy, "Wife Has Money". The house was very well positioned both to reach the ring road and therefore to get out to the rest of the diocese and also for walking home from the centre of Oxford after evening engagements. The only sadness about the house was that the Commissioners had not been able to buy the freehold and in due course it reverted to Wolfson.

Bishops are allowed a chaplain, a key appointment. When I was at King's I used to take groups of Ordinands to St Christopher's, the wonderful hospice founded by Dame Cecily Saunders who pioneered decent palliative care in this country. At the hospice I had met Jim Woodward who was doing a year working there before going to theological college. He used to talk to the ordinands about the work of the hospice and the kind of care they offered. I knew immediately he was the person I wanted and later managed to persuade him to move on from his curacy a little early, to join me. Jim is the most wonderful pastor and it has been a privilege to have him as a friend ever since. He is able both to be very affirmative and speak his mind. The only issue that emerged during his time as chaplain was when driving me one day he revealed he could not actually see very well; but that was put right when he purchased some glasses.

I was wonderfully well served by my five chaplains, Jim, Martin Gorick, Andrew Cain, Ed Newell and Michael Brierley, all very able people in different ways and a great pleasure to work with. I have been very blessed by their support and friendship. The office was at first more problematic. My predecessor was a saintly man, a very clever Scot with a nice sense of humour, but perhaps too saintly to be a good appointer of office staff. For the first few years I had to check everything myself very carefully before it went out of the office, and then Andrew Cain, a toughie who would not put up with this, brought about a change, and I had the superb team of Christine Lodge, first with Rosalind Beuzaval and then with Debbie Perry. Their great sense of humour was a real tonic, as well as keeping us all firmly related to reality.

People are sometimes surprised when I say it was easier to be a Bishop than a Vicar. Of course the responsibilities are larger and weightier. But as I mentioned earlier, if someone wanted to get hold of me they had to go through the switchboard, then the office or the chaplain or both. As a Vicar you live over the shop and people can call at any time of the day or night. Furthermore as bishop you have a prestige which means people treat you with a certain deference whereas as a Vicar you can, if you are unlucky, be regarded without the respect that once went with the position. So, from my point of view, there was a very happy, supportive and productive inner core to the work provided by the office team of chaplain, Christine and Debbie.

No less crucial, and arguably even more so, was the senior staff team. When I arrived, the Bishop of Buckingham was Simon Burrows. He had been appointed young and was expected to move on to a diocese of his own but, in army parlance, had been passed over. This could have made him bitter, or resentful of a new young Bishop of Oxford. But he could not have been more gracious or welcoming. In fact he was courtesy personified. When I arrived the Bishop of Dorchester was Conrad Meyer, who was strongly opposed to the ordination of woman, and who apparently did not get on well with my predecessor. He gave me a warm welcome but it was not long before he retired and then became Roman Catholic. The Bishop of Reading was Graham Foley, apparently a brilliant after dinner speaker who could earn £500 for a speech, a lot of money in those days. He had been Vicar of Leeds, traditionally a prestigious position, and he regarded it as a bit of a come down to be Bishop of Reading, a position he did not seem to enjoy and which left him behind his desk for much of the time, even when clergy came to see him. Again, it was not long before he retired, so I had the privilege of selecting two new area bishops, a wonderful opportunity for building my own team, their appointment being in my hands as the Diocesan.

As Bishop of Reading in 1989, I appointed the saintly John Bone, a long serving and much-loved priest in the Diocese, who was Archdeacon of Buckingham. I much shocked the serious minded John by simply sidling up to him one day at a church hall reception after some event and whispering in his ear that I would like him to be Bishop of Reading. John, an intelligent and devoted pastor was also meticulously well organised. As someone well said of him, "Love shone out of his filing cabinets."

The appointment to the vacancy of Dorchester exhibited the kind of system that operated in those days. One day at the General Synod in London I saw the Archbishop of Canterbury, Bob Runcie, writing a letter during a boring bit of business. It was addressed to me, asking me to consider Tony Russell for the vacancy at Dorchester. This was a very rural part of the diocese and Tony Russell was then the Director of the Arthur Rank Centre at Stoneleigh, which specialised in agricultural affairs. So I duly arranged to meet Tony half way between Stoneleigh and Oxford and we walked the fields together, totally avoiding the subject we both knew we had arranged to meet about. Instead I let Tony tell me about the various crops in the fields that we passed. But it was clearly an appointment for which he was well suited, for he was able to relate well to farmers and country folk generally, as well as the county set. Primarily a sociologist rather than a theologian, he had written an excellent book on the changing history and social role of the clergy. At staff meetings he brought a strong sense of where the natural strength of the Church of England lay and was therefore offered a critique of any artificial reorganisation that did not recognise this. One of his papers contained the important insight that "a small church is not a failed church". His natural ally in staff meetings was the Archdeacon of Oxford, Frank Weston, from a famous missionary family, who in due course went off to be Bishop of Knaresborough but who sadly died young. As Archdeacon of Buckingham I appointed another long serving and loved diocesan priest, John Morrison, before moving him on to be Archdeacon of Oxford.

In 1992 I needed a new Archdeacon of Berkshire. David Griffiths, a courteous man who had obtained a doctorate on different versions of the Book of Common Prayer, had retired. Jim Woodward, my chaplain at the time, had come with me to a service at a flourishing charismatic evangelical church where Mike Hill was Vicar. It was he who strongly suggested to me that Mike Hill was the right person to be the new Archdeacon, and how right he was. Mike, who comes from a North Country business background has a remarkable ability to relate well across all the traditional divides, and this is because in contrast to so many of us, he comes across as very real. In place of him as Archdeacon, I appointed Norman Russell, who had been a very successful vicar of St James's, Gerrards Cross.

When Simon Burrows retired I was clear in my mind who I wanted as Bishop of Buckingham. I had come across Colin Bennetts when he was the Vicar of St Andrews, a large Evangelical parish in which the bishop's house was situated. I knew how much the congregation valued his sensitive pastoral care as well as his preaching and leaderships gifts. He had gone off to the Chester Diocese and I was glad to get him back for the major job at Buckingham. Not surprisingly it was not too many years before he was appointed to a diocese of his own as Bishop of Coventry. There was an obvious replacement for him in the Diocese, namely Mike Hill, then Archdeacon of Berkshire. In place of Mike as Archdeacon, I appointed Norman Russell, who had a great capacity for hard, detailed work, and who later became the elected head clergyman of the General Synod.

When John Bone retired as Bishop of Reading I appointed Dominic Walker, a prayerful, disciplined priest of the Oratory of the Good Shepherd to succeed him. Then when he went on to be Bishop of Monmouth, I first tried to appoint Jeffrey John, which I discuss more fully later. When this did not work out, I was able to snatch Stephen Cottrell from under the nose of several other bishops who were keen to appoint him. Stephen, a great communicator, and a warm human being brought much energy into the senior staff team. To complete the team at that point there was Sheila Watson who replaced John Morrison as Archdeacon of Buckingham and Alan Wilson who came as Bishop of Buckingham, an appointment from within the diocese.

Sheila, married to my oldest friend, Derek Watson, combined serious strategic thinking with great attention to the detail on how this was to be realised. She should have been a Diocesan bishop but just missed out because of her age. Alan has an amazingly well stocked mind on a range of subjects with a lively turn of speech and is, amongst other things a respected blogger.

The Diocese of Oxford operates an area system. This means that the bishops I appointed were not just suffragan bishops, they had clear legally delegated responsibilities for their areas. As the areas of Buckingham and Berkshire were larger than a number of dioceses they were major jobs. The Bishop of Dorchester looked after rural Oxfordshire as well as keeping an eye on rural aspects of the diocese as a whole. The Bishop of Oxford is both the Bishop of the Diocese as a whole and the area bishop for Oxford itself. So the first important task of the Bishop of Oxford was to appoint good people to the senior staff. The record speaks for itself. Mike Hill went off to be Bishop of Bristol and Dominic Walker to be Bishop of Monmouth. Colin Bennetts went on to be Bishop of Coventry, Stephen Cottrell to be Bishop of Chelmsford and then Archbishop of York. Sheila

Watson, who had all the ability to be a diocesan bishop before legislation made women bishops possible became Archdeacon of Canterbury, the senior Archdeacon in the Church of England and then Chaplain of Lincoln's Inn. Train them up and send them on their way, I used to say. In fact of course I was as much trained up by them as they by their experience in the Diocese.

If the first task of a Diocesan bishop is to appoint good people, the second is to let them get on with it without inappropriate interfering. The Bishop of Oxford does of course accept engagements all over the diocese and will make a point of visiting every deanery but will make it clear that for clergy their bishop for all practical purposes is their area bishop. Dominic Walker, who had a wonderfully dry sense of humour, was apparently heard to say that the good thing about Bishop Richard was that he did not interfere in the running of the diocese, which I took to be a compliment. But then one of my mottos is that when in doubt take everything as a compliment, it helps ward off paranoia.

With our devolved area system clearly a key feature for the running of the diocese, we also enjoyed monthly staff meetings. We used to meet in one another's houses first for an early service of Holy Communion followed by breakfast, a morning's work and then lunch. We tried to avoid going into the afternoon except for something very special. Very important to the building of the staff team was the annual weekend that we spent away together, usually at a retreat house like the one at Burford. There, within a regular pattern of monastic prayer, we could try to think strategically for the year ahead. One custom, which was popular with most but not quite all the staff was the long walk across the countryside on the Saturday afternoon which I insisted on. This was followed in the evening, after one further work session, by a dinner with plenty of wine flowing.

I much enjoyed our time together as a staff and hope it was not too much of an illusion that the others did as well. We were serious of purpose, but convivial and there were plenty of laughs. The ethos of the meetings changed significantly about half way through my time at Oxford. It was probably true that for my first years there the other staff members were too deferential and did not challenge me enough. That was certainly not true for the last part of my time. Sheila Watson and Stephen Cottrell had strong views, not to mention Alan Wilson and Norman Russell who always had interesting or sound things to say. It became much more rumbustious, and no doubt healthy.

When I retired as Bishop of Oxford, people used to ask me whether I missed it. I replied, not at all, indeed a few days after I retired I had forgotten I had even been Bishop of Oxford. This is because I tend to move on and look forward and not back. Then after a few years of retirement I realised that I did indeed miss something and was glad to find that I was normal in at least missing something. What I missed was working as part of a team which was at once purposeful and convivial. By this I mean both the office team of chaplain and secretaries and the senior staff team. When one has retired, one is unlikely to be working as part of a team in that kind of way. I was hugely fortunate to be part of such a good one for so many years.

So what is the main role of the Bishop of Oxford? It is to give a sense of purpose and cohesion to the diocese as a whole. This very large and diverse diocese stretches from 20 miles north of Milton Keynes down to Windsor and Slough, and from near Swindon to the suburbs of London. I was helped in this by having a profile on the media but also I think by putting my energies into where I thought I, rather than anyone else, could make a difference. I was reinforced in this conviction by Charles Handy, the business guru, and an old friend, who kindly came to one of my staff meetings and spent the morning with us before sharing his reflections. He helped me to concentrate on what specially I could do, avoiding being distracted by other matters, in short, sorting out priorities. I was able, too, to get through a fair amount of work quickly. My predecessor had apparently written out every letter by hand before getting it typed and then checked. I used a small dictating machine and dictated scores of letters very swiftly. I was also strict about allotting time. Time for those who really needed it, an hour or more for clergy whom I was seeing for a regular assessment, but only enough time needed for routine matters of business and not more.

I was not only blessed in having a great senior staff team but both dedicated and able staff at Diocesan Church House and committed lay people helping to shape decisions. These decisions reflected the fact that even before I arrived the diocese was firmly committed to social justice. For example, when I arrived the Chair of the Diocesan Board of Finance was a local farmer who championed disinvestment from companies that had businesses in South Africa. It was one of those occasions when righteousness was rewarded, for at a time when shares fell steeply the money he had withdrawn was safely in the bank earning interest. The next chairman of the Board of Finance ensured that through a serious and very well organised fundraising campaign, the diocese raised more than a million pounds, a lot of money in those days, for the Church Urban Fund. Another example was the way the majority in the diocese was from an early period strongly committed to the ordination of women. Again, over the contentious issue of the parish share, the diocese consistently voted to ensure that all parishes were supported and we did not simply operate on a principle of parishes getting the clergy they could afford. Sometimes this feeling of solidarity was so strong that it precluded some people from realising as acutely as they ought the need to work towards financial viability in every part of the diocese.

Decisions on these issues were made at the Diocesan Synod and the Bishop's Council. I am not one for doing a great deal of structural organisation, believing that a lot of time and energy can be wasted to no good effect. But I did quickly bring about one change, which was to amalgamate the Bishop's Council and the standing committee of the Diocesan Board of Finance. The weakness I inherited was a Bishop's Council making policy decisions without taking into account the financial considerations. Under the change, it was the same people making both policy and financial decisions.

I have never been someone involved in the synodical process. I was asked to stand for Synod when I was on the staff of Wells Theological College, but at the same time I was given a major part in Anouilh's brilliant play *The Lark* and chose to do that instead, a choice I did not regret. So attending my own diocesan synod as bishop was the first contact I had had with the synodical process. "Enjoyed" is too strong a word to use about my chairing of this and Bishop's Council but both bodies were purposeful and I did not find it in any way a strain. Both bodies have the power to make important decisions. Deanery Synods, having no power, are the Cinderella of the system. Indeed, they have been well defined as "a group of Anglicans waiting to go home".

As to the staff in Diocesan Church House, at that time a converted vicarage in North Hinksey, I could not have been better served. There were some extremely able people there who could have earned much more money working for a secular organisation but who were totally dedicated to the work of the church. There was also a major workload with hundreds of church schools to administer, hundreds of vicarages to keep in repair and scores of churches every month wanting faculties for structural changes, including major re-ordering. What all this meant from my point of view was that I could have great confidence in what was going on. I knew that the legal documents that ended up on my desk to be signed had been thoroughly prepared and that good decisions were being made over a range of contentious issues. The officers of the Diocese were also forward thinking, sometimes anticipating developments that I was slow in gauging. One of the issues was the protection of children and vulnerable adults. As a result I believe we had a good system up and running early on. Another area was leadership development. Keith Lamdin was undoubtedly the ablest trainer in the Church of England who kept us ahead of the game on these issues. On a scale of leadership from one to five, with one being autocracy, the decision made just by the person at the top, to five, anarchy, with the decision being made by the group as a whole, I placed myself around three. I believe that a leader has to have some clear ideas of their own and in the end they have to carry the responsibility, but I also believed in maximum and genuine consultation, so that initial ideas could be modified, sometimes radically by those consulted. I suspected that Keith thought I ought to have moved more in the direction of five. Within the senior staff it was never one person's decision of course. The group was small enough to come to a common mind and did so on almost every issue.

It should be stressed that all members of the staff shared equally in the process of making decisions in the meeting. Traditionally bishops have been seen as dealing with pastoral matters and archdeacons with administrative ones. This is no longer applicable because so often it is the archdeacon who is most fully in the picture about the pastoral situation. No less valuable was the Diocesan Secretary, the person responsible for running the administrative side of the Diocese. Here again I was wonderfully well served, first by Terry Landsbert and then Rosemary Pearce. When on Terry's retirement I advertised for a replacement, I had about 70 applications, nearly all of them were from men who described themselves as consultants, no doubt having been made redundant at an awkward age. Rosemary came from running a national charity and was superb. Also at the staff meeting on an occasional basis was the Dean of Christ Church but there was no pressure for the Dean to attend. It was recognised that their main role was running the college.

Life as Bishop of Oxford was varied and interesting. Morning prayer in the room set aside as a chapel in Bishop's House was at 9 pm. This enabled the chaplain to come after the worst of the rush hour and then we could go into the office together. Before that there was good time for prayer, reading and any writing that needed to be done. Once or twice a week I went for an early swim in the University Pool. I discovered there an interesting social phenomenon. The men in their changing room developed a camaraderie that did not seem to exist to the same extent in the women's changing room. One sign of this was that when I retired, the group of regulars bought me a small toy swimmer with arms that moved, that now sits on my mantlepiece.

There might be a special engagement in the morning, such as the opening of a new church school or a visit to one of the 30 or so clergy chapters in the diocese. Otherwise it would be seeing people in the office and doing letters. Most bishops apparently like having their office in their home. I, by contrast, much enjoyed having it in Diocesan Church House. I appreciated the break between home and work but more than that it was enjoyable to have all the key officials handy to consult just by walking down the corridor. I just had to make it clear that it was the Diocesan Secretary, not myself, who was responsible for the administration of it all, and that was well understood. I tried to set aside one day a week for being in the Lords. A well worked routine was to leave the office about 12.30, drive rapidly round the ring road to the park and ride and then catch an Oxford Tube or X90, which dropped me at Marble Arch where I caught a taxi. I would usually be well in time for prayers at 2.30 and the afternoon's business.

There was often an engagement in the evening, perhaps some confirmation or special church event. There was also entertaining and being entertained. When we arrived at Bishop's House there was a very small inadequate dining room table. Instead of this I bought, out of our own money and through our dear friend Zal Davar, an antique dealer, a substantial mahogany dining table of about 1860 which could expand to seat 20. I am not a great one for possessions, but I loved that table and was sorry not to be able to take it with us when we retired. It provided a wonderful context for the dinner parties we much enjoyed giving. I read somewhere that in the church of the first centuries, church money was split three ways, one third to pay the clergy, one third to support the poor, and one third for the bishop to be able to offer hospitality. We did not cost that much, but it was nice to be able to have some paid local help with this entertaining.

The prime task of the Bishop of Oxford, as I have mentioned, was to give this large, unwieldy diocese a sense of cohesion and purpose. This was done partly by getting about the diocese for parish events and meetings of clergy. It also involved having a unifying theme in which our efforts could be focussed and our life in Christ revitalised. The main one that I initiated was called "Sharing Life". The prayer I wrote for this was:

Gracious God,
for the gift of life with all its struggle
and great opportunity
we give you thanks.

For Jesus the life giver,
in whom we have life with you
now and forever
we give you thanks.

For the Holy Spirit,
making us alive with his life
we give you thanks.
Open us to that Spirit
and renew your church,

that we may share your life with others.
Draw them into your love
and transform your world.

Another opportunity would be presented by the Diocesan
Conference which took place every three years. Traditionally
this would be for all the clergy and provided a great bonding
experience between clergy and bishops as well as a good learning
and inspiring experience. On the last evening there was usually
a revue in which the bishops and other aspects of diocesan life
were good naturedly lampooned. Early on, however, with all
the talk about clergy and lay people sharing together in the
ministry of the church we took the risk of having a conference
not just for clergy but lay people from all over the diocese. We
took over Butlins in Bognor for this. The thought of Butlins in
Bognor in February was not exactly appealing, but it turned out
to be the most amazing success. People arrived in good humour
and there was a truly remarkable spirit throughout, the work of
the Holy Spirit many of us felt. Sadly, next time round Bognor
was not available nor could we find anywhere else on that scale
suitable, so we decided to have a non-residential conference in
the grounds of Wycombe Abbey School over a long weekend. It
was well organised and there were a massive number of learning
opportunities which were well attended. But we definitely lost
something by not being residential. It is spending real time
together, relaxing as well as working, that matters. I believe
that when I left, the clergy hankered after the old clergy-only
conference with its camaraderie and cosy in-jokes.

There was the usual run of problems to deal with. I am glad
to say there was no child abuse scandal that I was aware of. We
did have one clergyman who combined a seriously disordered
mind with a fiercely litigious nature who took up a lot of time
and energy at one stage. There were the clergy who had really
given up and were just waiting for their pensions. One of the

difficulties with the Church of England is that clergy, even quite able ones, can get stuck in their parish. There may be no obvious job for them to go to, but they really ought to move on. Helping such people avoid bitterness and still minister faithfully was a challenge. Regular clergy appraisal helped but we never had enough resources to do this as it really ought to be done, for it is a time-consuming business.

One major initiative in my time was the serious leadership training for clergy running major parishes. This was extremely thorough, and involved the senior staff taking part as well, including the 360 degree appraisal. This includes reflections on how you are viewed by a range of others with whom you work. I found mine salutary, and I would, I am sure, have benefited by undertaking one many years before.

During my time there was a dramatic change in how discipline cases were handled. This can be illustrated by the case of Brian Brindley. Brian Brindley was a highly intelligent, flamboyant character of the kind who would not be ordained in the Church of England today. He was also Chairman of the business committee of the General Synod which required a particular kind of cleverness. As Vicar of Holy Trinity, Reading, he filled the church with every example of Victorian Anglo Catholic accoutrement, including a Ruskin reredos. When I took part in a service there to celebrate his twenty-fifth anniversary as a priest, he ordered me a purple zucchetto from Gamarelli's in Rome, dressed me up in amazing togs and set me on a peacock throne.

Brian was returning from a do in London one night with a reporter who had a microphone on and who got him to talk indiscreetly and lewdly about various relationships. This appeared in the newspapers. The first instinct of a bishop in those days was to protect someone who had been betrayed like that, so I drove over to Reading to offer him some support, and this included a bottle of gin. Although I was definitely not in favour with friends of Brian because of my support for the ordination of women, I earned a brownie point with them for that bottle of gin. The scandal lingered on until leading evangelical members of the General Synod issued a public declaration that Brian Brindley should resign, which again received a great deal of publicity. I was then warned privately by a member of the press whom I trusted, that there were more stories in the pipeline about Brian. I had no alternative but to call Brian in and confront him with this, at which point he resigned. He became a Roman Catholic and hit the headlines again when he died in the middle of a seven-course dinner he was giving for his seventieth birthday at the Athenaeum – between the dressed crab and the *boeuf en croute*, as the papers put it.

Now, of course, and rightly, a bishop would have no alternative but to suspend a priest as soon as an allegation has been made, though in that case there was no actual allegation.

Life as Bishop of Oxford was not all work. In the summer there was the occasional luxury of an afternoon's game of tennis on the well-kept grass courts in the University Parks with a number of university don friends, not least the splendid Jack McManners, the historian and chaplain of All Souls College, whose father had been a Durham miner. I also played on the Wolfson Courts next door to our house in Linton Road with the President, Bill Hoffenburg, a great man who was deeply involved in the struggle against apartheid in South Africa. Walking was also a great pleasure, round Port Meadow with lunch at one of the pubs, in Wytham Woods or along the Thames tow path. Especially for me there has been the Chilterns, in particular the part around Turville, which both before our time in Oxford and until the time of writing I love. I have always thought of this area as God's own country. We also had a few interesting parties with some of the residents there, especially John Mortimer who liked to call himself the founder of Atheists for Christ.

There was one bizarre event that involved this group of Chiltern writers and actors. The old Church School in Turville was due to be sold, so a group of people, led by John Mortimer, got together to raise money to buy it and turn it into a centre for children from inner cities to get some experience of country life. However, opposition in the village was stirred up and when I came with John Mortimer and others to launch the fundraising in the school, the narrow road leading to it was lined with villagers who clearly wished they had scythes in their hand to cut us down. One of the leading opponents, an aggressively rude woman, told me at a party in the village that there would be too much noise from the centre. This was a centre that would cater for a dozen or so children for a few weekends a year. I rather relished the remark of Roy Jenkins about this lady. "Yes, I have never quite seen the point of her."

II. The ordination of women

I was always instinctively in favour of the ordination of women and when the debate intensified in the 1980s, I put together an open letter to Graham Leonard, the Bishop of London, who was the leader of the opposition to women's ordination. I did this with two leading Jesuits, a senior Anglican Evangelical and two other senior Anglicans. The theological grounds for opposition always struck me as weak. It depends on believing that the male gender of Christ is an essential feature of the divine revelation. I do not believe it is any more essential than his being Jewish. What is essential is the personhood of Christ. It is this which the priest represents at the altar, not his maleness. The ecclesial grounds for opposition was much stronger. This depends on the belief that the Church of England claims to be part of the Catholic Church, and therefore should not go it alone without the consent of the greater part whose allegiance is to Rome, or Constantinople. This argument had more force in the 1960s when the hope of some kind of rapprochement with Rome was much more hopeful. But by the 1980s it was clear that Rome had no real will for reunion on any terms that the Church of England would find remotely acceptable. So it was a question of two competing claims, the one of eventual church union, the other of the clear call of many women to ordination. At the Reformation the Church of England made changes that 400 years later the Church of Rome also made, for example, having the service of the church in a language that people could understand. I believe that eventually the Roman Catholic Church will accept the ordination of women. When change does come in the Catholic Church it comes fast. As has been said, "What Rome forbids today it commands tomorrow." And as the joke has it, "At the next Vatican Council the Bishops will have their wives with them and at the one after that the Pope will have her husband." My open letter did not have an Orthodox signatory but I remember the highly revered Metropolitan Anthony of Sourozh saying to me in private that he did not see any fundamental theological objections to the ordination of women.

The Diocese of Oxford was overwhelmingly in favour of the ordination of women and it was clear that this was coming for the Church of England. But how could the position of those who were opposed be respected and contained within a church that had women priests, and indeed later, women bishops? This continued for a long time to be the key question. The decision was eventually made for alternative or extended episcopal oversight. There would be a Provincial Episcopal Visitor himself opposed to the ordination of women who would offer pastoral care of priests and parishes who remained opposed. But the contentious issue was whether this should be an entirely separate stream, as it were a church within a church or a generous extension of the Diocesan's responsibility. Two factors were decisive with me. First, David Hope, Bishop of Wakefield then London, and afterwards Archbishop of York, was a member of my episcopal cell group. So the question for me was a very personal one. Did I want to make such provision as to keep David within the Church of England or force him to leave? The second was a House of Bishop's meeting at which the much respected John Habgood, then Archbishop of York, who was regarded as an arch liberal and strongly in favour of the ordination of women, argued in favour of alternative episcopal oversight. In fact I remember checking him and insisting on using the word extended rather than alternative. But the point is that the Church of England did eventually make provision to keep the vast majority of those opposed within its life, not of course without much pain to women priests who would find their ministry rejected by a number of priests and parishes. At the crucial General Synod Meeting on the issue, a lay woman from the diocese of Oxford who had been elected on an antiordination of women ticket changed her mind on the issue and abstained, thus allowing the vote in favour to go through. I can still see her sitting forlorn and isolated in her seat in the hall as everyone else went through the doors to vote. A few priests became Roman Catholics. In fact, the best of the priests we lost to Rome did not usually do so on this issue, certainly not this issue alone, and some of those who converted we were relieved to lose. The major difference that the Ordination of women has made is that the whole church now feels a much more healthy institution. I now find it uncomfortable to be in a meeting which is all or nearly all, men.[23]

III. Church traditions

The Church of England contains a number of different ecclesiastical traditions. The bishop is of course the bishop of everyone, however they define themselves. But not everyone will regard him as their bishop. For many centuries the typical Church of England parishioner would attend an 11 am morning prayer on most Sundays and make their communion twice a year at an early service. By the 1960s this kind of pattern had mostly gone.

First, because of the liturgical movement which brought the Eucharist back into the centre of church life, people were both encouraged to receive communion regularly and to do so at the main Eucharist on a Sunday morning. The name itself, meaning thanksgiving, was significant, getting away from the old divisive nomenclature of the Mass, the Lord's Supper and the Holy Communion. The second reason was that many people wished to identify with either the Evangelical or Catholic wing of the Church of England. The Catholic wing in its modern form is a fruit of the Oxford movement, which saw itself as heir to those reformers who stressed the continuity of the Church of England with the pre-reformation church. Until recently it was the dominant ethos of the Church of England, particularly its leadership, as represented, for example, by Archbishops Michael Ramsey and Bob Runcie and later, Rowan Williams. Unfortunately in recent decades this Catholic wing was radically divided between those in favour of the ordination of women and those who are opposed. This has been one of the reasons for the weakened position of the Catholic element in the life of the church.

The evangelical wing again traces its root back to the reformers and in particular the Calvinist elements in the Book of Common Prayer, both in the services and the 39 articles. But more particularly it is the heir of the evangelical revival at the end of the eighteenth century, and more recently of the missions of Billy Graham in the 1950s, and the long and influential ministry of John Stott at All Soul's, Langham Place. They have been represented in leadership more recently by Archbishops Donald Coggan and George Carey.

Evangelicals have been growing in strength and influence in recent years to the point where they are now the dominant force in the church today. This is because of the number of ordinands that have come from this tradition and because evangelicals have been much more serious and innovative about addressing the issue of mission in our present secular culture.

To these two main tendencies we must add two other features. One is the word liberal which includes the acceptance of historico-critical methods of studying the Bible as well as an acceptance of some social developments, certainly the ordination of women, and for many, same-sex partnerships. The other is charismatic renewal, which can influence congregations and denominations of all traditions but is in fact mainly a factor in evangelical churches. So it is that we have open evangelicals and charismatic evangelicals and distinguished from both those two, conservative evangelicals who are strongly Calvinistic in their theology, uneasy about historico-critical study of the Bible and opposed to liberal social changes on the ordination of women and same-sex relationships.

I related perfectly happily to the vast majority of parishes in the diocese but two traditions found my ministry difficult or unacceptable. One was that composed of traditional Anglo-Catholics who opposed the ordination of women. This would be manifested in the fact that when I visited such a church there would be a picture of the Pope in the vestry and a card asking for prayers for the provincial episcopal visitor, the bishop appointed to care for those opposed to the ordination of women but not for me as their Diocesan bishop! The other group were the conservative evangelicals, who insisted that a bishop other than myself performed their confirmation. Within Oxford were two very flourishing Evangelical churches. St Aldate's was charismatic. They always made me most welcome and I much enjoyed going there. On aesthetic grounds, the terrible music and lack of any prayerful stillness meant I could not worship in such a tradition regularly but I really enjoyed doing so on such occasions. There was also St Ebbe's which was conservative evangelical in its outlook, for whom my ministry was unacceptable. As far as the two most famous high or Catholic churches in Oxford itself are concerned, Mary Mags appointed a priest who was in favour of women's ministry during my time, whilst St Barnabas, though opposed to women's ordination in principle, actually supported women ordinands from the parish and welcomed my ministry.

IV. Religious Communities

One of the distinctive features of the Diocese of Oxford is that it contains most of the religious communities in the Church of England. This is not surprising because the revival of the religious life in the church was a direct result of the Oxford movement. As Bishop of Oxford I was visitor to about half a dozen of these communities, all of whom were experiencing a decline in vocations leading to the possibility of moving into more modest accommodation or even amalgamating or closing. Some of the sites were magnificent like Parmoor the old home of Sir Stafford Cripps overlooking the Hambledon Valley where, when I arrived, one ancient nun hung on. A vivid example of the change experienced by these communities is that of the Community of St John the Baptist at Clewer, Windsor, (just near my old prep school). In its heyday it had some 450 nuns. The story is told of Queen Victoria visiting and standing talking to the Mother Superior. Whenever a nun went by, they curtsied. Queen Victoria turned to the Mother and said, "I thought I told you that this was to be a private visit," to which she replied, "Don't worry Mam, they are curtsying to me not to you." The Community sold its vast buildings and moved into a remodelled Roman Catholic Community in Begbroke just outside Oxford before this again proved too large and they moved to the College at Cuddesdon, resulting in building an award willing chapel there.

It was a heroic task for such communities, not only facing the normal challenges of maintaining a religious vocation but having to live with too large premises, no new vocations, and an increasingly elderly community, many of whom needed much nursing and thinking through how they should manage the future. As Visitor to these communities I was expected every few years to conduct a major visitation over several days with the help of a small team. Every nun was given a personal interview and every aspect of life looked at as we tried to help them both keep up morale and plan for a realistic future.

For my own personal quiet days I used to go to the Priory at Burford, where there was a mixed community of men and women which held up quite well. They too eventually found their building too much, however, and moved to a specially designed ecologically friendly building in another part of the country. Oxford itself had two religious communities, The Sisters of the Love of God at Fairacres being an enclosed, contemplative one. Before my time as Bishop there had been a very influential Mother Superior, Sister Clare. She relates how her vocation came to her. She was nursing in Cardiff during World War II at the height of the bombing of the docks. She felt a strong conviction that the front line of the battle was not in the air between the allied and German planes, nor even in the docks where she was tending the wounded. It was a spiritual struggle. So it was that she decided to enter a contemplative order, that is one wholly given over to prayer. I much enjoyed my contacts with all the communities and found them very warm and welcoming.

V. Public Schools

Another feature of the diocese is that it seems to contain half the public schools of England including Eton, Radley, Wellington and Bradfield for boys, and Wycombe Abbey, Downe House, St Mary's, Wantage (which later merged with Heathfield), and Queen Anne's, Caversham for girls. The area bishops and I took it in turns to confirm at these schools and I was the Visitor to a few. The heads were often very serious Christians, as were a number of members of staff and the chaplains struggled heroically to bring the faith alive to their pupils. But by then the whole culture of the country had changed and this was inevitably reflected in the attitude of parents to such schools and what they wanted from them, and this of course rubbed off on their offspring. Shortly after becoming Bishop, I visited Radley. The much revered Warden, as the headmaster of Radley is called, was Dennis Silk, a serious Christian, who also had five blues. I said to him that that Radley, which had once produced so many ordinands for the Church of England was now producing virtually none. "Oh, Richard," he said ruefully, "the whole concept of service has gone." It was a time when many of the brightest and best who would previously have gone into the Foreign Office or Civil Service were going into merchant banking or acting as corporate lawyers.

I did my best to take these confirmations seriously. Some were quite exhausting, such as Eton, which involved the whole weekend. But this brought the pleasure of being the guest of some wonderful Provosts such as Martin Charteris and Anthony Acland who always gave a great dinner party for the confirming bishop on the Saturday night.

VI. Universities

When people hear the title "Bishop of Oxford" they immediately think of Oxford University. In fact there are at least five universities in the Diocese and another in Oxford itself, Oxford Brookes. It is important for the Bishop to keep that in perspective. It is also important to keep Oxford itself in proper perspective. As a Cambridge graduate myself, with my wife and wife's family having been educated there and later with both son and grandson as graduates, I was not likely to be overawed by Oxford. Furthermore having been Dean of King's College, London, I was aware of the number of Nobel prize winners who came from a London University and this helped to put Oxbridge itself in proportion. So I went to Oxford at ease with the place, not trying to recapture the glamour of a youth spent there or wanting to ask of it what it would not give anyway. The academics, all experts in their own fields are independent minded, as are the colleges in relation to the university. Being a head of a house, as being head of a college is called, remains a highly prestigious position but it is not an easy one. The head has very little power over the governing body of fellows and has to tread very carefully. A number of national reputations quickly floundered on the rock of such governing bodies. The story is told of one candidate for a headship receiving a letter from the clerk to the governing body which began "After a long and stormy meeting the governing body has instructed me to invite you to be principal of the college."

I enjoyed my relationships both with heads of houses and academic staff more generally. One remarkable feature of my time there was that amongst the strongest supporters of their college chapels were the three highly distinguished Jewish heads of house. There were some excellent heads of houses, some of whom I like to think of as friends. But it is sad when, as sometimes happens in colleges, the massive minds and formidable intellectual energy of some members of a governing body became focussed on some relatively minor but divisive issue.

VII. The Queen, God bless her

I was a teenage republican. In those days the National Anthem was played at the end of every theatre and cinema performance. I had furious rows with my mother when I refused to stand as she did. Later, I underwent a genuine intellectual conversion to monarchy. I can remember the exact spot and occasion. It was when I was chaplain of Westfield College at a reception held in summer on the lawn. I was in conversation with Norman St John Stevas, an ardent monarchist, and he convinced me that the monarchy was the great unifying symbol in our society now. I have never been emotional or sentimental about royalty but I believe that what Norman St John Stevas said then is still true and I have the utmost respect for the way the Queen has carried out her duties so faithfully over so many years. One of her acts of hospitality is to invite every Diocesan bishop once in their time to spend a weekend with her at Sandringham. You arrive on Saturday afternoon and after briefing and a cup of tea, go to your room where your clothes have been laid out and your bath run. Then there are drinks and dinner at which you sit next to the Queen. I was advised to choose either horses or the Commonwealth, about which the Queen knows a great deal, as subjects of conversation. After dinner there was the choice of going into the sitting room with the Duke of Edinburgh and members of staff to watch a film. As keeping up conversation in a royal context is something of a strain, I chose this as the easier option. It was I think the worst film I have ever seen. It was also a black mark. For when I emerged from this terrible film there was the Queen and the Queen Mother busy doing a jigsaw puzzle. I realised that this was the option I should have chosen.

Sunday morning at breakfast was bizarre. I sat next to Princess Diana, gorgeously arrayed in a white trouser suit, for it was at a time before the split, and all the family were there. On a nearby table were all the Sunday papers with the usual salacious gossip about the Royal Family.

The bishop has to preach at the 11 am service of morning prayer in Sandringham Church, which is one of the reasons he is invited for the weekend. After the service various people gathered round a local lady who had read the lesson rather well, including the Queen. "You weren't listening, Bishop," she said. Second black mark. I had indeed been having a surreptitious glance at my notes before going up to preach, which the Queen had noticed and remarked on. "I was doing both, Mam," I replied.

After lunch and various activities in the afternoon, including some shooting for those who wanted it, I left with a pair of unplucked pheasant. In fact they were very cheap in the shops at the time and it took Jo quite an effort to pluck them. But how gracious of the Queen to share her weekend so generously and gracefully with every Diocesan bishop in this way.

Cumberland Lodge, situated in Windsor Great Park, played a part in my life for some years. As Dean of King's, I used to take 70 new students there every year for a weekend just before they started their course. I was also involved in the planning of two conferences. One was on soap operas. I managed to gather a group of writers, producers and ethicists to think about the ethical dimension of soap operas. I wanted them to think about the main kind of moral messages which were being conveyed by their storylines. I did not imply any critical judgement by this. I just wanted them to reflect on the fact that whether they knew it or not certain implicit moral values were being conveyed, and these might be very good ones. Sadly too many of those most directly involved still understood the words ethical and moral in very narrow terms, as referring only to sex. The other conference was concerned with religion and the media. What brought it about was the feeling in all religious communities that they are not being reported fairly or accurately by the media. It is a concern that has not gone away.[24] I was also a trustee of Cumberland Lodge and this meant I had opportunity to meet the Royal Family on various occasions, especially the Queen Mother who took a very personal interest in the Lodge.

A most memorable occasion in connection with the Royal Family was a major banquet at Windsor Castle for Nelson Mandela. As always the Royal Family was very gracious in making everyone feel at ease and there was a conducted tour after dinner to see interesting exhibits in the library. It was quite a treat next morning for Jo and I to wake up and find the walls of our room studded with Canalettos.

In the army the toast was always "the Queen, God bless her". Yes, indeed, says this converted monarchist.

VIII. Prime Ministers

Writing about the Queen followed by Prime Ministers reminds me of a Dean of Windsor who once remarked to a friend, "The Queen and I don't like name droppers." But the country residence of Prime Ministers, Chequers, is in the diocese of Oxford, and this brought me, as Bishop, into contact with some of them. At a time when the relationship between the government and the Church of England was very low, Mrs Thatcher kindly invited Bob Runcie and a small group of bishops for lunch and discussion with her at Chequers. When I came through the door into the sitting room, the Prime Minister, who was standing at the far end, greeted me with the words, "Ah, the Bishop of Oxford. I listen to you on the radio. Sometimes I agree with you and sometimes you make me mad." Then, all charm, she asked me what I wanted to drink. My unconscious, clearly unsettled by this beginning, came out with the answer, "Perrier water, please, Prime Minister," even though I had never asked for Perrier before in my life. "We don't serve Perrier water in this house, Bishop." was the stern retort.

In the discussion after lunch Bob Runcie outlined how he saw the relationship between the Church of England and the then government in his usual amiable style. Very quickly Mrs Thatcher followed, opening with the words, "I don't think it is quite like that, Archbishop." A lively discussion followed. It ended in prayer but no meeting of minds.

When John Major was Prime Minister he kindly invited Jo and myself to Sunday lunch. I was immediately impressed by the way he greeted us as we got out of the car with our Christian names. It was an interesting gathering, composed mostly of his boyhood heroes like the cricketing twins the Bedsers. I sat in a small group with John Major himself, the Chief of the Defence Staff and Joan Hickson, who played Mrs Marple in the TV series based on the stories of Agatha Christie. When young, John Major had once been laid up in bed for many months with a serious illness, he had devoured the books of Agatha

Christie, remaining a great fan. The main reason I remember the occasion, however, is because of my discussion with the Chief of Defence Staff. I was very concerned at the time about what was happening in Bosnia and believed strongly that there should be an armed intervention by Britain and others to stop the atrocities. The Chief outlined all the military obstacles, with Serb forces occupying the high ground, and so on, which were indeed real. But I felt that behind this analysis there was no political will and the Foreign Office was obtaining the military advice it wanted to hear.

John Major never went to University which was perhaps one of the reasons which helped him to think in an uncluttered manner. He once said that if he had a big decision to make he drew a line down the middle of the page and on one side put down all the reasons for one course of action and on the other side all the reasons against. Interestingly Charles Darwin adopted the same technique. In the middle of one of his scientific notebooks there is a page marked marriage, with a similar line down the middle. Amongst the reasons against was "terrible waste of time". Amongst those in favour was "companionship, better than a dog anyway".

Jo and I twice went to dinner with the Blairs at Chequers. The guests were a little different from those of John Major, composed mainly of people who were then making their mark in different areas of life like the inventor and manufacturer James Dyson and the Paralympic athletic winner Tanni Grey-Thompson. On one occasion Jo sat next to Chris Evans, with whom she got on well. On both occasions I sat next to Cherie Blair when we had serious discussions about religion.

I was from the first sympathetic to Tony Blair's political vision. Ever since I started to think politically I have been situated broadly on the right of the Labour party. Tony Blair's willingness to accept the free market but to try to make it work for everyone, especially those who were losing out, seemed to me the most realistic approach to achieving greater social justice in the modern world. Described as the third way, after a book of that title by Tony Giddens, it was not as vacuous as some supposed and his governments had real achievements to their credit. A greater degree of privatisation was not incompatible with this goal of greater social justice provided the state remained firmly in control of what was happening. One thing which went very badly wrong, however, and which precipitated the financial crisis was the extent of deregulation. Regulation of markets is fundamental to reining in the excesses of capitalism.

The other reason I was sympathetic to his position was his liberal interventionism. I believe that the international community, through the UN, does have a duty to protect when there is a real threat of genocide or massive human rights abuses on minority groups. This instinct of Tony Blair led him to press for two justified interventions, one in Kosovo and the other in Sierra Leone. Alas, his third, in Iraq against Saddam Hussein turned out to be a tragic misjudgement. I was opposed to that war because I did not believe it fulfilled the criteria of a Just War, but I do not think it was a criminal or ignoble decision. And the main reason it was disastrous was the failure to plan properly for the occupation itself. I suspect that if this has been planned properly and the country better governed and policed after the invasion, some of those who are now loudest in their condemnation of Blair would have been calling him a hero.[25]

It was a pity that Gordon Brown did not have longer time as Prime Minister, due significantly to a bad misjudgement over the timing of an election. A person of massive intellect and strong moral conscience, he hugely impressed the Bishops of the Church of England when he addressed them. He did a heroic job rescuing the international financial system after the crash in 2008. However, in what must be one of the biggest "cons" in political history, the Conservative Party managed to load the blame for the financial crisis on the alleged profligacy of Labour spending and Labour was amazingly weak in countering this at the time. Since retiring Gordon Brown has been a prophetic voice on a number of major issues.

A favourite memory is a party given by Barbara Castle at her house Hell Corner Farm in Ibstock. In addition to Gordon Brown and his wife, Sarah, there was only Jack Straw and his wife, Alice, Mary Wilson and Jo and myself – only those who had the fierce Barbara's seal of approval!

IX. Social Responsibility

My case against the Church Commissioners was heard in 1991. Even before that, however, I had been concerned with the wider area of both ethical investment and social responsibility. Ethical investment, that is, taking ethical considerations into account when deciding what to invest in, was regarded as very much a fringe idea in those days. Those of us who championed the idea, however, argued that it was an idea whose time had come. Events have proved this judgement correct, as the significant percentage of shares now managed on the basis of this principle, now termed socially responsible investment, shows. At that time people tended to take the view that it was legitimate to invest in any company on the stock exchange, and the understanding of "ethical" in some minds was a very narrow one. I found it difficult, for example, as a trustee of Cumberland Lodge at the time to get the idea taken seriously. The fact is that this is a very grey area in which discrimination is needed and there are no perfectly clean hands. The present Archbishop of Canterbury, Justin Welby, discovered this when he called on the church to set up credit unions in opposition to the high street lender Wonga because of the very high rates of interest they charged. Then it was discovered that through an investment company in which the Commissioners had a small stake, they did in fact own a very small percentage of Wonga shares. But that kind of difficulty ought not to stop a serious attempt being made to bring the investment of money into the moral realm, and for the Christian, into their discipleship.

Although we lost the case against the Church Commissioners, in the sense that the Judge did not make the declaration we wanted, as was mentioned earlier, he did make some highly significant points. First, it is legitimate for trustees to take ethical considerations into account. What is not allowed is to do so if the result would be significant financial loss. Secondly, it is legitimate to disinvest from a company, even if the result is loss, if the investment is in a company whose purpose is at odds with the purpose of the charity. For example, a cancer charity should not invest in tobacco shares even if these were highly profitable. Then, thirdly, it is legitimate to disinvest from shares if as a result of holding them the charity would lose the financial backing of its supporters.

Disinvestment is not of course the only option, and many shareholders now prefer to raise issues of concern with companies directly, as does the Church of England's Ethical Investment Advisory Group. A major concern now, quite rightly, are environmental issues. The Ecumenical Council for Corporate Responsibility considers the whole issue more widely on behalf of all the churches.[26]

In 1993 the Royal Institute for Arts and Manufacturers launched a widespread consultation under the heading "Tomorrow's Company". The result of this was a serious championing of the stakeholder concept. Instead of companies being responsible to shareholders alone, it was argued that companies have a responsibility to a range of people, all of whom have a stake in it. These would include suppliers, customers, employees and the wider community in which the company operated, as well as shareholders. As a result of my involvement with this project I found myself speaking to a number of gatherings of business leaders. I enjoyed bringing before them the guiding principle of a major American retail company.

"The business of business is serving society, not just making money. Profit is our reward for serving society well. Indeed profit is the means and measure of our service – not an end in itself." The opening sentence of that principle immediately roused people's hackles, but I hoped that by the end, when they had pondered the rest of the paragraph, it made sense. The problem of course is that whilst this might fit well into a manufacturing or retail company it is difficult to see how it could include the daily manipulation of the financial markets using mathematical models or the chronic short termism which has beset British business for too long.

Business is the great engine of society and needs to be affirmed but it is driven by human beings and therefore like everything else human has an ethical dimension which we neglect at our peril. I tried to convey this twin sided approach in a project I did with Sir Hector (later Lord) Laing the Chairman of United Biscuits and a leading layman in the Diocese of Oxford. We produced a simple booklet, which was widely distributed, titled *The Value of Business and its Values* which set out the stakeholder concept in simple terms.

In recent years more and more companies have in theory adopted this approach and company reports more often than not appear with a mission statement boldly set out stating how the company sees its obligations. But there is all the world of difference between a mission statement that has been dreamt up by the chairman in their bath and promulgated from on high and one which has been widely discussed and endorsed by the company at every level, and which includes a realistic way of monitoring its effectiveness. We also have to bear in mind that large companies spend large sums of money on public relations exercises and, particularly where environmental or community considerations in the developing world are concerned to create a positive image even though dispassionate observers might tell a very different story.

These concerns about investment and social responsibility were brought together with my earlier work on Christian attitudes to wealth, poverty and the economic order in a book titled *Is there a Gospel for the Rich?*[27] This is a genuine, not just a rhetorical question because the Bible makes it clear that the kingdom of God belongs to the poor. If that is so, what is the good news for the rich? How could there be good news when Jesus said it was easier for a camel to go through the eye of a needle than for a rich man to enter the kingdom of God?

It is a question that has quite properly troubled the Christian conscience whenever the church has faced up to the issue. How the church responded in the period 350–450 was particularly brilliantly recounted by Peter Brown.[28] My starting point was the question of what was meant by the term "the poor" in the Bible. Does it refer to material poverty or a spiritual attitude of humility? My conclusion is that it refers to the devout who put their trust in God, even though they lose out in the world as it is now. In other words it is a word that brings together both a spiritual attitude and the material circumstances of the person. It is this person who is above all the subject of the psalm one of the *anawim* the devout poor. I found the work of Charles Elliott helpful in thinking about the application of this when he argued that often the best way of helping the poor of the world is not by going to where they live and helping them physically but by raising questions in our own society about the kind of political and economic policies which may be contributing to their poverty. And the implication of this for me is the need for a sense of solidarity with those who lose out in the world as it is now. It is making that solidarity a reality that we become one of the poor who are blessed. A story is told of Mrs Thatcher visiting Liverpool with her husband and listening to a sermon by a Methodist minister who used the word "solidarity". Apparently, Dennis turned to her and said, "I don't think that is one of our words, is it, dear?" But for a Christian it surely ought to be an important word. I summed up my thinking on these lines in a prayer at the end of the book.

Risen, ascended, glorified Lord,
Grant that I may be in such solidarity with those who lose out now
That I too may be one of the poor whom you pronounce blessed:
And grant that I may so stand against the forces that crush the powerless,
Looking and working for your new order of love,
Trusting in you,
That even now I may be filled with the richness of your presence
And know the glory of your kingdom.

As a Bishop I attended meetings of the House of Bishops, presided over in my time first by Bob Runcie then by George Carey and Rowan Williams, though the actual chairing was often shared with others, especially the Archbishops of York. The House of Bishops used to meet residentially in different parts of the country. I particularly enjoyed meetings in Liverpool where we stayed in the Britannia Adelphi Hotel. This was a magnificent building, complete with spacious rooms, marble walls and fine woodwork where the wealthy stayed before they caught one of the great liners plying the Atlantic in the 1930s. But by the 1990s it had become very run down and indeed the subject of a lampooning TV programme. With its reduced status and sense of faded grandeur it seemed a very fitting place for Church of England bishops to have their meetings! Liverpool also offered the redeveloped docks with the Liverpool Tate, and a brisk walk down from the hotel there through the cheerful, chirpy Liverpool streets.

My main role, however, within the wider circles of the church was as Chair of the Board of Social Responsibility which I was from 1996–2001. Before the cuts, when it became incorporated within the Board for Mission and Public Affairs, it had a number of specialist staff so it could do good thoughtful work in the range of areas for which we were responsible. It was presided over by the excellent David Skidmore, a former University lecturer who combined a keen eye for detail with a gloomy prognostication about the prospects of the Church of England. Our task was to respond on behalf of the church to various government consultations and provide reports to the General Synod on the major issues of the day, as well as be the church's voice on some of the items in the news when they impacted on our sphere of concern. It was a role for which my academic background and interests had provided some preparation, and I was very glad to serve in this way.

My last senior staff team. Left to right: Michael Brierley, Alan Wilson, Rosemary Pearce, Norman Russell, Me, Sheila Watson, Stephen Cottrell, John Morrison, Colin Fletcher.

Chapter 17

Jeffrey John and same-sex relationships

When Dominic Walker went off to be Bishop of Monmouth I appointed a committee to advise me on the appointment of a new Bishop of Reading. This was unusual at the time, most bishops reserving the appointment of suffragan bishops exclusively to themselves. We shortlisted four candidates, one of whom was Jeffrey John. I rang up Rowan Williams to inform him that I was doing this and he made no particular comment. At the interviews it was obvious that Jeffrey was the outstanding candidate, a gifted teacher and a prayerful caring pastor whose Catholic spirituality fitted what we needed at that point. I was of course aware of his excellent booklet arguing that the church should fully accept gay people and also that he was in a partnership. However, he affirmed that this had been celibate "for a considerable period". No less important for me was the fact that during his time in the Diocese of Southwark he had become much admired by evangelicals for his Gospel teaching and commitment to mission. Philip Giddings, a leading evangelical layman both in the diocese and on General Synod, who was a member of my advisory group expressed hesitations but no one strongly disagreed. I rang up Rowan to tell him I wished to nominate Jeffrey. Surprisingly quickly, he agreed.

When the news got out a strong campaign against the appointment was mounted by so called Anglican Mainstream. They unearthed a paper that Jeffrey had given some years before which contained some outspoken remarks on gay relationships and gave it wide circulation on the internet. I was put under huge pressure to withdraw my nomination. This included a meeting with a dozen leading evangelicals from the diocese. It was the toughest meeting I had ever experienced. The meeting was at St Ebbe's church where, some years later, the able Vicar bravely came out publicly that he was sexually attracted to men. On Saturday 5 July 2003 at 8 am both Jeffrey and I, having been duly summoned, appeared at Lambeth Palace and went in separately to see Rowan and told that he was not prepared to go through with the appointment. I was shattered and wanted to resign in protest as a matter of principle. Poor Jeffrey had it much worse with his house being staked out by the press and a trawl being made through the land registry to see if he and his partner owned a property together.

I have never blamed Rowan for this and continue to hold him in the highest admiration. I can see that in his role as Archbishop he had to try to hold both the Church of England and the Anglican Communion together. Where he went wrong was in agreeing to the nomination too quickly, being led to do so by his instinctive support for, and known positive views about, gay people, his admiration for Jeffrey, and no doubt pressures of work. We clearly should have met and thought through where opposition would come from and whether, when it came, we could hold firm to the decision. The debacle was caused by his agreeing to the appointment and then withdrawing his approval. I had anticipated opposition from within the Diocese of Oxford but believed that within two years Jeffrey would have won the trust of evangelicals as he had in Southwark. What we had not anticipated was the pressure that could be brought from around the world by a well organised email campaign. I suspect it was Anglican Mainstream who also arranged for a letter to appear in *The Times* from a number of Church of England bishops opposing the appointment, which was a breach of collegiality without precedent. Later, Rowan said that this opposition from other Church of England bishops had been the main influence on his decision not to go ahead with Jeffrey's appointment.[29]

This episode changed me. Although I had been liberal in my views about gay people before this, afterwards it became a matter of deep conviction that they be treated equally and that the church fully accepts them.[30] One consequence was that it made me unequivocal in my support for legislative changes such as the equal age of consent, civil partnerships and gay marriage. I spoke and voted in favour of all of them as the legislation went through the House of Lords. What I have really wanted from the first is that the Church of England would fully accept civil partnerships and allow Clergy to bless them. However, when the legislation on civil partnerships went through parliament it was opposed by the bishops, even though later they backtracked on this somewhat and suggested they had supported it. It would in my view be quite acceptable at the moment to leave the traditional definition of marriage as it is but allow civil partnerships to be blessed. I supported gay marriage on the grounds that gay people wanted it and felt that if it was not open to them civil partnerships would be regarded as a second best option. In fact according to the theology of the Church of England the marriage bond is created by the couple making vows to each other before witnesses. It is not the presence of a priest which makes it a sacrament. So we have to ask in what way are such partnerships not a marriage? So my main concern continues to be that the clergy be allowed to bless such partnerships, even if at the moment the church cannot bring itself to offer an official liturgy which would be preferable. Since then I am glad that both the Church in Wales and the Episcopal Church of Scotland have accepted gay partnerships and are willing to have them blessed.

Jeffrey John was rescued by the Prime Minister's patronage office and made Dean of St Albans, where he has been outstanding. Very sadly he has been blackballed for a number of other episcopal appointments, including most recently the

Diocese of Llandaff which was 100% in favour of his appointment. Disgracefully, the Welsh College of Bishops refused to consider his appointment apparently on the grounds that they were too exhausted to cope with any ensuing row that might result.

Chapter 18

Life with their lordships

There are 26 places for Bishops in the House of Lords. The Archbishops of Canterbury and York, and the Bishops of London, Durham and Winchester take up their seat on consecration, the others wait until there is a vacancy due to retirement. This usually means a wait of 4–6 years, a useful period to get on top of the Diocese before taking on wider responsibilities. I took my seat in 1993 after consecration in 1987.

It is very difficult for bishops to make a serious contribution to work in the House of Lords not just because of their Diocesan Commitments but because their engagements are usually fixed long in advance and cannot be changed at short notice. Business in the Lords, by contrast is often not fixed until two or so weeks beforehand. Furthermore for the second reading of a bill and some other business you have to put your name down to speak in advance and you have to stay until the end, which means 10 pm at the earliest. If a Bishop is coming from afar this means at least two days in London. I decided therefore that the only thing to do was to set aside a regular day to be in the Lords, whatever the business, and this is the advice I give to new bishops. How often that day is will obviously depend on how much of a commitment they want to give to it. I tried to give one day a week. As stated in an earlier chapter, I could work in my office in the morning and be there for the start of business at 2.30 and be back in Oxford not too late even if I stayed to the end. Furthermore, with an area system it was much easier to make myself free for this. One reason for giving at least one day a week to the Lords is that unless you go in regularly you don't really keep in touch or know what is going on. As so often in life it is the chance meetings and encounters in the corridors that keep one informed about what is going on and therefore better able to make a sensible contribution.

In addition to what the Bishop himself may be able to provide in the way of research resources, there is a solid team, once based at Lambeth and now in Church House, which keeps bishops well informed and briefed for particular debates. It is important not to exaggerate the influence of Bishops in the Lords, they are simply not able to give the necessary time to it. As the late Lord Hailsham once remarked, "Bishops blow in, blow off and blow out again." Nevertheless the presence and contribution of bishops is respected and welcomed by the vast majority of peers.

Two of the most controversial bills when I first came into the Lords were the Hunting Bill and the bill to expel hereditary peers, who at that time numbered many hundreds, even though only a small percentage turned up. As the House at that time did not finish at 10 pm as it does now, sittings could sometimes go on all night. The bill to get rid of hereditary peers gave rise to one of the most powerful speeches I heard in my time, from Lord Williams of Mostyn then leader of the Labour Party in the House and Leader of the Lords. Summing up towards the end he said:

I promised, when I responded to a complaint that I had said something unworthy, to return to what the noble Lord, Lord Inglewood said. He described his pride in his family, in history and in public service. I respect that. I honour it. I know him well and I think he would identify himself as one of those I described earlier. He said of his ancestors and relatives, quoting Yeats, "they are no petty people". Perhaps I may explain why some of us have a slightly different view of society, history and tradition.

My own father was a village schoolteacher. His father was gassed in the First World War and could not, therefore, work properly thereafter. His father, my father's grandfather, remembered the evictions in West Wales of tenant farmers because they voted according to their consciences in parliamentary elections before the secret ballot Act of 1870 was passed. They were evicted from their homes and their farms and many of them had to emigrate. They were back country people. They lived unremarked, though not unremarkable, lives, and I take up the noble Lord's words, of duty and service. There are millions like them in our country today. All I would say is this: "they are no petty people".

That is a small illustration, just a tiny cameo – and forgive me my indulgence this late at night – but I am entitled to say, as long as I can breathe, that I am proud of their service and duty, but equally I do not look to them for any advantage in this world, except their memory. I do not look to them to have provided me with any personal or political advantage. I believe it would demean them and demean me similarly.[31]

As I am a descendant of Welsh farmers on the Dynevor Estate it brought tears to my eyes, but also made me wonder if my forebears had been as brave as those of Lord Williams.

I contributed to a range of issues over the years, no doubt without much effect in the world of events but there was one which did have a lasting impact. This was the Embryology Bill. Here my influence, such as it was, can be traced back to an academic paper by Gordon Dunstan. Dunstan, by training a medieval historian, had become one of the country's leading ethicists with a particular concern for medical ethics. In this learned article he traced the church's teaching on the embryo from the church fathers and canonists to our own times. He showed that for most of its history the church made a distinction in the moral status of the embryo depending on whether the abortion was early or late. Abortion was always a sin but the punishment prescribed was very different depending on the stage of development of the foetus The doctrine that an embryo has the full moral status of a human person from the moment of fertilisation came from Pope Pius IX in 1869 and did not really represent mainstream teaching before this. I took this line in a speech on the bill and no doubt as a result of this was asked to chair the House of Lords Select Committee on the subject. The key issue was whether scientists should be allowed to develop stem cells from embryos. The Government were in favour but as it was a highly contentious issue they felt that extra reassurance was needed. I am under no illusions that I was asked to chair the committee because as a religious leader who was likely to be in favour of the bill, this reassurance could be provided. We had a distinguished committee which was a real privilege to chair, and two excellent scientific advisors who taught us the basic facts of human embryology. It included two Roman Catholics who, with appropriate wording, felt able to support our recommendations despite the teaching of their church. It was the work with this committee that led to me being invited to be a member of the Human Fertilisation and Embryo Authority. Here we worked at the ethical and legal cutting edge and were able to authorise such procedures as preimplantation genetic diagnosis, which prevents a hereditary condition being passed on to the succeeding generation. My very able colleagues included people like Sir Simon Jenkins, Emily Jackson, the Professor of Medical Law and Ethics at LSE, and Sharmila Nebhrajani, capable of running any organisation however large. All remain good friends. After this I served on the Nuffield Council on Bioethics. My work on embryos in the Lords also resulted in me being elected an Honorary Fellow of both the Institute of Medical Research and of the Institute of Biology. Wonderfully bogus when you think that I don't even have an O-level in biology.

The average age of members of the House of Lords is high. Ann Mallalieu in one of her speeches recounted how early in her time there she was sitting at the long table when in one of those silences from the far end were heard the words "Why are all my lovers dead?" at which point an elderly peer at the far end stood slowly up and said, "What about me?" The equally elderly peeress peered at him for some time before replying, "I thought you died years ago."

There are also some great characters there. One of my favourites was Norman St John Stevas who earlier in my ministry had converted me to the idea of monarchy. His final home was a penthouse flat just round the corner from the Lords which he wanted because he could see both Westminster Abbey and Westminster Cathedral from there. His flat was studded with signed photos of the Royal Family and memorabilia of Rome and the Popes. It had its own oratory complete with a reassembled Pugin reredos. One day in a debate on public transport Norman got up and in his distinctive languid tones said that he always travelled by public transport because "I want to give the public an opportunity to view me". My favourite story about him concerns the time when he was in the cabinet of the Prime Minister he dubbed "Blessed Margaret". At one point he put up his hand and apologised to the Prime Minister that he would have to leave early for another event. When she asked which event it was and he told her, she said, "But I am going there too." To which he responded, "Yes, Prime Minister, but it takes me longer to change than you."

One of my favourite memories from the Lords is of Ruth Rendell and P.D. James warmly embracing in the chamber before they went to vote in different lobbies. Belonging to different parties, writing different kinds of detective stories, yet united in mutual affection and a shared Christian faith.

The most controversial issues as far as the Church of England is concerned have been those concerned with legislation in relation to same-sex relationships. First there was the question of the age of consent. The key vote on this happened during the 1998 Lambeth Conference, so it was agreed that about eight of us should attend, split more or less evenly for and against, reflecting the division in the House of Bishops. Bishops in the House of Lords are not mandated by the Church of England and use their own judgement but of course take seriously any policy that the Church might have. The second issue was that of civil partnerships which the church opposed. By that time I was a Life Peer, and was able to speak freely in support.

I was a member of the Royal Commission on House of Lords reform chaired by Lord Wakeham which produced its report in 2000. John Wakeham, a former Chief Whip in both the Commons and the Lords is a canny and kindly operator, with a great sense of humour about the skills he uses to get things through without too many ruffled feathers. He was a fund of amusing stories of how he had gone about his business. He was determined that we produce a report that would be put into effect. The members of the commission represented different points of view as well as different professions. Douglas Hurd, a clever and decent man who should have expressed the Conservative position at that time for an elected house was not very forceful in putting it forward. The enigma on the commission was Gerald Kauffman, who allegedly was not a fan of Tony Blair but who, I suspected, had been put in by Blair for some purpose. Anyway we had no difficulty about agreeing certain fundamentals, such as the separation of the honour of a peerage from automatic membership of the Upper Chamber; 15-year terms of office with renewal being only a rare occurrence; a statutory appointments commission which would oversee not only cross bench appointments but political ones as well, and a maximum size of 450. The number of bishops were to be reduced to 16 and their places taken by leaders of other Christian denominations and other faiths. Where we had difficulty was whether we should be all appointed or elected. Eventually we settled on a compromise, whereby there would be a tranche of elected members, and their number would gradually increase over three elections to compose half the house. My preference would be for a wholly appointed house but I supported this compromise not because I thought it would be more democratic, which I do not believe, but because I thought it would give a greater chance for people outside London to be members. The report was rejected by nearly all parties because none of them were prepared to compromise or have a hybrid house.

Since then there has been total stalemate. We desperately need reform, not least in our numbers which are grossly more than what they should be. But those in favour of a fully elected house tend to oppose incremental changes for fear it would in the end undermine their case. But I believe, with John Wakeham, that something along the lines of what we proposed will eventually be accepted except for the elected element. In reality it is only the Liberal Democrats who are totally committed to an elected house. The Tory and Labour party pay lip service to the idea of an elected second chamber but a high percentage of their members in parliament do not in fact want it. However, there is another factor now with the existence of the Scottish parliament and the Welsh Assembly. We could get a very different kind of second chamber in which the four nations are represented in some formal way. This might become a very live option if the UK became seriously in danger of breaking up.

In recent years the Lords themselves, frustrated about the progress of reform, proposed a system of at least reducing numbers. Some Lords die each year, others retire. It was agreed that there should be two out for every new one in. But in the end this depends on the Prime Minister of the Day agreeing to this. There has not been much sign of this.

When I retired as Bishop of Oxford in 2006, I lost my place in the Lords as, unlike other peerages, Lords spiritual are not there for life, only for such time as they are a diocesan bishop.

A number of people, however, were very keen for me to stay on and an application was made to the appointments commission for me to be made a cross bench peer. What eventually happened is a mystery. What I guess happened, and it is only a guess, is that the appointments committee did not want to nominate me for fear of setting a precedent for retired bishops and also the number of places they have vacant in any one year is tiny, with hundreds of applicants to consider. In the end I received a letter from the Prime Minister, and I think I must have been offered one of the places that is reserved for the PM, which go to people like the head of the civil service, the head of the foreign office, the Chief of the Defence Staff and so on. I am grateful to the people whoever they were, whose voices in the right quarters made this happen. It has been a good experience to stay on in all kinds of ways.

As referred to earlier there was something of a farce over my *Nomen dignitatum* which the Garter King of Arms said I had to have because Harries was too like Harris. Wanting to make reparation for the fact that I do not speak Welsh, I thought the least I could do would be to be Baron Harries of Ceinewydd and this I duly registered. But when I got home there was a riot from Jo and Isabel, her sister, who know it as New Quay. So I rang up the Garter King of Arms and asked if I could change it. He told me it had already gone to the Queen which of course it hadn't and made a great fuss about calling over his secretary to check. Anyway, when I went in again to sign a new set of papers he did not seem to press the question too hard about whether Pentregarth was a proper place. Just as well, because as mentioned earlier it is simply a row of five cottages. So now I am Baron Harries of Pentregarth of Ceinewydd in the county of Dyfed. There was also a dispute about whether Ceinewydd was spelt with one word or two. The local council spell it as two, and the county council as one. So I decided to get a definitive ruling from the Lord Lieutenant.

As a retired bishop who is a life peer I have my own unique form of address. In addition to the noble and learned lords, the noble and gallant lords, the right reverend primate and right reverend bishops there is me as the noble and right reverend lord. Or to give him his full title the Right Reverend Dr Professor the Honourable Lord Harries of Pentregarth! How wonderfully absurd, and how good now to be known just as Richard Harries.

On more serious matters in addition to the usual business, I have focussed on a number of human rights issues. One is the Dalits, the former untouchables who by every criteria: lack of clean water and sanitation, poverty, rape, sexual trafficking and access to justice suffer disproportionally in India and other South East Asian Countries. There are 240 million Dalits in the world, a fair number of them being part of the Asian diaspora in the UK. There is clear evidence of discrimination against them even in this country and after a number of years of pressing we managed to pass an amendment which had the effect of making discrimination in the public sphere, that is in education, employment and the provision of goods and services illegal. It would join race, gender, religion etc. as a protected characteristic. Those taking the lead on this issue in Parliament were the late Lord Avebury, Lord Lester and Jeremy Corbyn, though it was I who proposed the amendment in the Lords that brought about the change. Unfortunately, sections of the Hindu community clearly had the ear of David Cameron and for years they successfully blocked the implementation of the Act, even though it has been passed by both Houses of Parliament. At the time of writing the government have stated their intention of repealing the amendment. I have been vilified in the Hindu press, even though we have stressed all the way through that this is a social phenomenon which has affected all religions including Christianity.

Another human rights issue to which I have been committed is West Papua, the western part of the Island of which Papua

New Guinea is the East. Originally under Dutch control it was invaded by Indonesia and 1020 handpicked men were "largely coerced", to use the phrase of a British Foreign Office Minister, to agree to integration into Indonesia. Since then, there have been massive human rights violations with neither the press nor NGOs able to enter and travel in the country. As Bishop of Oxford I was called upon to support various worthy causes and one of these concerned what was happening in West Papua. I was so impressed by the integrity and perseverance of Benny Wanda, the West Papuan spokesman in this country that I, together with Andrew Smith the MP for East Oxford, did our best to support his cause, regularly raising questions in parliament. I am glad to say that over the years this once unknown struggle has gradually climbed up the international agenda. The first aim must be to get the UN, who played an unfortunate role, to re-examine what it did in relation to the misnamed "Act of free choice" in 1969 which was in fact an act of no choice. This was a gross historical injustice which must be lanced.

Another area of concern in which I have been involved is the role of charities in society. When the Lobbying Bill came before parliament, Part II concerned charities and third-party organisations. A group of more than a hundred of these felt that the proposals there would seriously inhibit their capacity to campaign at election times. These groups were of every kind of persuasion from the Countryside Alliance to Friends of the Earth. They felt that the main umbrella group for charities, the NCVO was being too acquiescent in these proposals and they therefore decided to set up their own organisation, The Commission on Civil Society and Democratic Engagement, to oppose them. I was asked to chair. In a remarkably short time a significant sum of money was raised and a tiny highly efficient staff assembled. Third parties were regularly consulted and their views formulated in a series of reports and then amendments to the bill. As a result the bill was improved in a number of important ways. One amendment ensured that the working of the Act, when passed, would be monitored. This was done by Lord Hodgson after the last election. He made a number of major recommendations, which had been argued for by the Commission but not accepted by the government when the bill was going through parliament. In fact other issues have taken over, and these recommendations have not been implemented. It was a good experience to work with such energetic and efficient people from the Third Sector and experience how a difference could be made. One example was the petition they produced with something like 200,000 signatures which I was able to show in one of my speeches in the Lords only a few days after it had been initiated. It brought me up into the reality of the digital age.

Another issue I have been involved with is divorce law reform. The Church of England has sometimes been too slow in recognising needed changes in the law. Occasionally, however, it has pioneered the way. The idea of irretrievable breakdown as the sole ground for divorce was first put forward in an authoritative document by a Commission set up by the then Archbishop of Canterbury, Michael Ramsay, and chaired by the then Bishop of Exeter, Dr Robert Mortimer, in 1966. Irretrievable breakdown was incorporated in the 1973 Act. Until recently, however, the existence of that breakdown had to be shown by the evidence of one or more of five facts, three based on conduct, adultery, behaviour or desertion and two relating to periods of separation: two years if both parties consent and five years without consent.

In 1996 that remarkable man James Mackay brought his Family Law Bill before this House. It sought to do away with the establishment of one or more of the facts as evidence of the breakdown, and also gave the couple an opportunity to think again about their marriage through the use of relationship support services to see whether it might be saved and, if not, whether mediation might provide a better way forward. I strongly supported this bill, against fierce opposition from some Christians. It was passed but not implemented by the incoming government and eventually repealed. Together with James MacKay, I strongly supported the 2020 Divorce, Dissolution and Separation bill, which again was based on the concept of irretrievable breakdown but required no evidence of this apart from a signed statement of one of the partners. Though supporting the bill, I argued for more prominence and support being given to relationship support organisations and also a statement in the bill that the present legal understanding of marriage had not been changed as a result of the Act.

One thing tends to lead on to another, and I have served on a House of Lords Select Committee concerned with charities, excellently chaired by Jill Pitkeathley. Then on another one on Citizenship in which it was a privilege to observe David

The Royal Commission on the reform of the House of Lords.
Standing left to right: Baroness Dean, Lord Butler, Professor Dawn
Oliver, Kenneth Munro, Professor Anthony King, Ann Benyon, me,
Bill Morris (later, Lord Morris), Sir Michael Wheeler Booth. Seated
left to right: Gerald Kaufman MP, Lord Wakeham, Lord Hurd.

Introduction to the House of Lords, with Julia Neuberger and David Wilson.

Blunkett bring his knowledge and passion to bear. These committees were in contrast to the Joint Committee of the Lords and Commons I had previously sat on, concerned with privacy and super injunctions. We sat at the same time as the Leveson Inquiry and saw the same witnesses, but the whole process was highly unsatisfactory.

The House of Lords does essential work in getting the Commons to think again and as a result improving so much legislation. But at the moment it is under attack on the grounds that it is too large and there are too many peers there who do very little or nothing but who still draw a full daily allowance. I think this can only change when we have reformed and are reduced to about 450, so that those who are appointed would expect to play a much larger role rather than just turning up to support their party in the lobby.

Chapter 19

Georgia

The reason for including a short chapter on Georgia is that I have been fortunate enough to visit this remarkable country at a number of crucial points in its recent history. I have been left with fond, vivid memories of the country, its turmoil and its people, which have helped to shape me. I have also tried, over the years, to raise questions in the Lords on Georgian issues. In order to see where my visits fit into the rapidly changing political circumstances of the country, this is a timeline. On the left is the name of the regime or ruler. On the right is the nature of my visit, IPU standing for Interparliamentary Union.

Georgian timeline
Part of the Russian Empire
1918–21 – Democratic Republic
1921–1990 – part of Soviet Union, 1984 – visit with peace trip
1991–2 – Gamsakhurdia
1992–2003 – Shevardnadze, 1993 – visit with George Carey
1997 – visit with Arthur Peacock
2003 – Rose revolution
2004–13 – Saakashvili, 2011 – IPU visit
2008 – war with Russia
2012 – Bidzina Ivanishvili, 2012 – visit for Europe Week enters
    politics with Georgian Dream, 2014 – IPU visit
2021 – Mikheil Saakashvili returns from Ukraine where he has
    been in exile and is imprisoned.

My first visit to Georgia was in September 1984, when I was Dean of King's College, London. This was part of a peace delegation to the Soviet Union, which included visits to

Moscow and Estonia, which I mentioned briefly in an earlier chapter in relation to Russia. In Georgia, the first memory which remains is of the extraordinarily lavish hospitality, the like of which I have not encountered before or since. It may have been the height of the Cold War, but the Georgians knew how to do themselves well. On a heavily loaded table, one course followed another, washed down with innumerable toasts of vodka, brandy and wine.

The point of our visit was to see a State Farm which in itself offered nothing significant to our untrained eyes. It was the dinner afterwards which was so revealing. We were only a small number in our party, the farm manager, the chairwoman of the local communist party, the young male secretary of the party, and two local doctors. What interested me was the question of where power lay. One thing was obvious, the doctors did not count. Rather, they tended to be the butt of jokes. They may have been the most educated people there but they had no leverage in this gathering. It was clear that the old farm manager, a war veteran, was hugely respected. The older lady chair was also highly significant, but was she more powerful than the mostly silent young party secretary? I could not quite make up my mind, and still cannot, but I suspect that if the crunch came it was the secretary; but that for day-to-day purposes it was the farm manager whose word went.

My next visit to Georgia was in the first week of May 1993, when as Bishop of Oxford and with special responsibility for trying to co-operate with the Russian Church in particular on practical help in matters of ministry, I went with George Carey the Archbishop of Canterbury. In addition to our time in Georgia, we spent time in Moscow and Armenia. Flying by Aeroflot was an unnerving experience, not just because of the lack of basic comforts in the plane, but because the plane might be very delayed, having moonlighted on some private trip, run out of petrol and put down elsewhere to refuel.

This was a key moment in Georgia's modern history. As Foreign Secretary, Eduard Shevardnadze had made many key decisions in the Gorbachev era. In 1992, after the turmoil following the breakup of the Soviet Union, he became President of Georgia. George Carey, myself and Stephen Platten, who masterminded the trip, had a formal meeting with the president. Half way through the meeting Patriarch Llya II came into the room to present the President with an Icon. It was the first anniversary of his Christian baptism! Apart from any matters of personal belief, Shevardnadze would have wanted to identify with his people. It was not an incident we could imagine happening in number 10, but it indicated the continuing importance of religion in Georgia.

It was an uneasy time in Georgia's history. Although Shevardnadze had taken over and would give the country a period of relative stability, it was still volatile. We went to sleep at night to the sound of occasional gunshot, and Mrs Shevardnadze admitted to us she was terrified. As well she might be, as later there were attempts on her husband's life.

A major figure on our visit was the Patriarch, the most revered figure in Georgia's recent history, who had become a symbol of Georgia's independence of mind under Soviet domination. He received us most graciously. Visits to dignitaries there are very formal affairs. The Patriarch sat in a large chair in the centre of a stately room and we sat around him with a cup of tea in our hands. Conversation consisted of a polite question via an interpreter to which the Patriarch would give an uncontroversial response. After the questions, a Georgian Orthodox choir sang beautifully for us, and we received the Patriarch's blessing.

One vivid memory is of the Patriarch leaving the palace and saying goodbye to his beloved dog, the watery eyes of both looking into each other soulfully. In due course the Patriarch paid an official visit to England and we entertained him at Bishop's House in Oxford.

I admired the way George stood up for his wife, Eileen. On our first day in Georgia when we were collected in a fleet of black cars and George was seated in the front one, he later found out that Eileen had been displaced from the front by Orthodox hierarchy and put in a back car. He was furious and insisted that on future journeys she should be near him in the front.

Another vivid experience of Georgia was my visit in 1997 when I travelled with Arthur Peacock and our wives, Rosemary and Jo. Arthur gave a lecture at Tbilisi University on Christianity and Science and I gave one on Christianity and Art. It was a time of the most extraordinary contrasts. On our trips around the country we could see the rusting ruins of heavy industry, for the economy was totally devastated. We heard of one professor at the university who had to live on his state salary of £1 a month and died of starvation. At the same time I have never seen students who were smarter dressed. Instead of jeans and T-shirts, the students wore black shoes and well-cut black clothes with fashionable handbags to match. There was also the extraordinary phenomenon of a concert given by the Moscow State Orchestra. They flew in, late of course, but the concert was packed with people paying the equivalent of £50 for a ticket. Clearly, although there was dire poverty, a black economy flourished in some quarters.

We were looked after by Tamara Grdzelidze, who interpreted and guided us. We were lucky enough to have a hired car and driver for more than a week and were able to visit some of the main churches and historic spots in Georgia.

In 2003, after the so called "Rose Revolution", Shevardnadze resigned and Mikheil Saakashvili became President. In 2011 I went as part of an Interparliamentary Union delegation with three MPs and another peer. As a result of the 2008 war with its neighbour, Russia had not only occupied Abkhazia and South Ossetia but was camped barely twenty miles from Tbilisi, the capital, just about the distance of Windsor from London. We visited the "line of control" and could see Russian soldiers moving about just the other side. The country was full of refugees who had fled from Abkhazia. At the time of writing that situation still prevails.

We visited Stalin's childhood home in Gori where his father ran a shoe shop until it failed. A very modest house with shop front on the street. We also visited the Museum of Stalin, outside of which his statue still stood. At the entrance was a health warning about Stalin's atrocities. Just as well, as inside the museum was given over to celebrating his early life as a revolutionary in Georgia. We also inspected Stalin's train. Because of his fear of flying he went everywhere in his train, so we could see his bedroom and study.

During our visit we met many members of the United National Movement, Saakashvili's ruling party, which was very Europe and NATO orientated, and contained many able people. This was during Saakashvili's second term in which the economy began to flourish and much endemic corruption was eliminated.

In 2012 I was invited to give a lecture in Tbilisi as part of their Europe Week. This was especially memorable for reasons unconnected with the official gatherings. On previous visits I had got to know Malkhaz Songulashvili who is officially a member of the Baptist Church in Georgia. In fact, his outlook is really reformed Orthodox and he dresses and thinks very much in Anglican ways. He is a serious scholar, with a doctorate from Oxford, and has translated the Bible into Georgian. But it is his public ministry which is so remarkable, standing up bravely for women bishops and gays and against all forms of religious intolerance. On one occasion he was severely beaten up by thugs from an Orthodox monastery and had to go to Germany for treatment. Malkhaz became a good friend, staying with us in Oxford and Wales. On this visit to Georgia we went for a walk together in the spacious and beautiful countryside. On the way he rang up friends of his to arrange a meal for us. Here, in a very poor home, we received simple but lavish hospitality, including slugging wine down from great beakers made of horn. We then had to speed back to Tbilisi, where the President, Mikheil Saakashvili, was giving a banquet in our honour. I sat at his table where he switched easily between French and English. He had discovered it was my birthday, so in addition to the official speech he got up later and made a second speech in my honour, presenting me with a small replica of the Georgian lion, one of their national symbols. It was such an extraordinary contrast between the banquet in the magnificent new presidential palace overlooking Tbilisi, and the very simple home where I had been entertained earlier. What united them of course was the same warmth and generosity.

This visit gave me more time to walk about Tbilisi, a most attractive city, especially now the ancient houses with their balconies, which I first saw in a dilapidated state, have been carefully restored.

My last visit to Georgia was in 2014. It was a puzzle why Saakashvili lost the election in 2012, when shortly before he had such public ratings. The reason appears to be that he had stamped out corruption, including sacking the whole police force, for which he won international plaudits. Shortly before, the election scenes had been shown on TV of some of those in prison being badly treated. As almost everyone in Georgia had a friend or family member who had suffered in this way, the country very quickly turned against him.

In 2012 the wealthy business man Bidzina Ivanishvili entered politics and founded the Georgian Dream party, which has been in power ever since Saakashvili lost the election and resigned. There have been a number of presidents and Prime Ministers since then but it is in fact Bidzina running things from behind the scenes. In 2021 Mikheil Saakashvili returned from Ukraine where he had been in exile and was put in prison where he still is. This has included a hunger strike of more than fifty days. Sadly, the

Russians still occupy much of the country and their influence is strong in some quarters.

Our visit this time in connection with Georgia's ambition to join the EU was not only to Tbilisi but to Batumi, on the Black Sea coast. This is very different from the rest of Georgia and is built up, quite attractively, as a holiday resort and magnet for gamblers from Turkey and Iran. Sadly, I have not been able to go to this wonderful country since then but it is lodged firmly in my heart and mind.

With Bob Runcie, the Archbishop of Canterbury, and Luis Prado, Bishop of Pelotas, at an Anglican meeting in Singapore.

In Georgia, with Ala and Malkhaz Songulashvili.

Chapter 20

Seven archbishops of Canterbury

I have known seven archbishops of Canterbury – in varying senses of the word "known", of course. This is a personal reminiscence, and only that. No attempt has been made to see those discussed in the round, write mini-biographies or weigh their legacy.

In the 1960s and '70s when the World Council of Churches had greater financial resources and more influence than it does now, it created an international furore over its programme to combat racism (PCR). This was a period when liberation movements, particularly in Africa, were struggling to overthrow their imperial masters, and the PCR included support for the non-violent and humanitarian aspects of their struggle. When I was on the staff of Wells Theological College, a letter of mine supporting the PCR appeared one day as the lead letter in *The Times*. The retired Archbishop of Canterbury, Lord Fisher of Lambeth, wrote me a strong letter opposing my position and invited me to where he lived, not far from Wells, to discuss the matter. I took up his offer and we had a robust discussion followed by another letter from him restating his disagreement with me.

Geoffrey Fisher (Archbishop from 1945–1961) had been a public school headmaster and he still had that manner. Robert Stopford, later Bishop of London, told me that once at a meeting of Bishops, Fisher was acting in this way when he, Stopford, dared to put up his hand and say, "Excuse me, sir, we are all headmasters now"! Fisher was an extremely able man, with a string of first class degrees and he applied his intellect and formidable energy to sorting out the Church of England after World War II. It is as an able administrator that his reputation rests. But I had another wider view of him when I was working on his papers at Lambeth Palace on the 1956 Suez crisis. Fisher was deeply suspicious of the Government's policy and intervened in the debate with the simple question "Who then was the aggressor?" I find it impossible to imagine anyone in the Lords now putting such a question in such a way more than twice at the most. Fisher interjected with the same question eight times. Lord Hailsham who led on this issue in the Lords was furious and a vigorous correspondence between the two in their own handwriting ensued. Both were highly intelligent, belligerent men who combined aggressive candour and steely politeness in equal measure. The correspondence went on for some time until Fisher wrote an eleven page closely typewritten letter on large A5 paper setting out the theological basis of their different approaches to the issue. The exchange was finally closed when Fisher did not reply but wrote down that Hailsham would never give in, and anyway he was mad! What is most interesting, however, is Fisher's serious intellectual grappling with the general question of what was appropriate for a church leader to say in such circumstances. In the letter[32] he said that he and Hailsham had "quite different conceptions to the principles which ought to guide an Archbishop in discharging his duties".[33] His own starting point is the duty of obedience to God. "It is the ceaseless task of the Christian and the Christian minded state to strive after that one obedience." There are two interesting points about that sentence. First, the reference simply to "the Christian", a reference that would include both Archbishop and lay person, and that lay person in both their private and their public role. Secondly, the phrase "Christian minded state". It implies, in a rather careful way, that the state, as a state, is to strive after that one obedience. It is doubtful if now our multifaith society would be receptive to this kind of language, but the Archbishop felt it was still appropriate in 1956.

So, there is "one obedience", but the Archbishop then goes on to say that the government, which of course Hailsham was representing, and he as Archbishop, approach this from opposite ends. The Government is concerned with the temporal ends of the society it governs, but he as Archbishop is concerned, referring to God, "to relate what I can perceive of his perfect will to our temporal affairs... that is my special contribution". He said that, starting from different ends it is not surprising that they do not come to an exact meeting point. When that is the case "it is our duty to call to each other so that we may help and warn each other".

Fisher then quotes Temple to the effect that we can only look at issues properly if we can exorcise self-centeredness, but interestingly applies this not to the individual case, but to public policy. A government will inevitably look at issues from a national perspective. He, as Archbishop will look at them from a much wider view, and he reminds Hailsham, rather sharply, that he has duties not only to the nation, but to the wider world, and in particular to the wider church at home and abroad. Which leads again to his emphasis on referring the matter to the UN as a way of approaching that wider perspective.

This letter is very revealing, and although Fisher is not usually rated as a theologian, it seems to me that his understanding of the respective roles of politician and church leader, and how they might approach the issue, could hardly be bettered. What we note above all is that whilst there is a tension there is no absolute dualism. There is a proper difference of roles, a genuine tension, but no abyss between the two.

Fisher retired in 1961. He advised the Prime Minister, Harold Macmillan, that he did not consider Michael Ramsey, who had been his pupil at Repton, a suitable successor. Ramsey later told Victor Stock the conversation Fisher had with the Prime Minister.

According to this account, Fisher said, "I have come to give you some advice about my successor. Whomever you choose, under no account must it be Michael Ramsey, the Archbishop of York. Dr Ramsey is a theologian, a scholar and a man of prayer. Therefore, he is entirely unsuitable as Archbishop of Canterbury. I have known him all his life. I was his Headmaster at Repton."

Macmillan replied: "Thank you, your Grace, for your kind advice. You may have been Doctor Ramsey's headmaster, but you were not mine."

Ramsey was duly appointed and was Archbishop from 1961–1974. This was during my time as an ordinand at Cuddesdon, a curate at Hampstead Parish Church and then a lecturer at Wells Theological College. He was very much an Archbishop for people of my ilk, a serious biblical scholar, a man of prayer, a Catholic in his churchmanship but genuinely open, for example, to reunion with the Methodists, liberal on social issues and left of centre politically. That stance very much represented the leadership and main body of clergy in the Church of England at the time. Stories about Ramsey's lack of small talk are legion, as are those at the time who could mimic his manner of speaking but where he was really at home was in answering theological questions either in private or in public meetings. Here he was in his element. I cannot say I knew him well, but I saw him in action at such gatherings and was impressed by the lucidity and prayerfulness of what he said. He was very much the teacher. Archbishop Ramsey was also around in Oxford living in retirement for some of the time when I was Bishop, where his presence was much enjoyed by local residents. A little earlier when he lived in Cuddesdon he enjoyed playing croquet with the students and a friend tells me he was ruthless at it, showing a guile and subtlety that belied his shambling mannerisms and holy reputation.

During the 1960s and '70s many Christians were critical of the positions being taken by the World Council of Churches in their programme to combat racism. The distinguished American ethicist Paul Ramsey voiced some of their views in his book *Who Speaks for the Church*?.[34] In that book he held out as a model of the kind of statement the church should make what Archbishop Michael Ramsey said in relation to the Unilateral Declaration of Independence by Ian Smith the Prime Minister of what was then Southern Rhodesia. The Archbishop wrote to Harold Wilson, the Prime Minister, to say:

If notwithstanding all efforts there shall come a breakdown and if you and your government should judge it necessary to use force to sustain our country's obligations, I am sure a great body of Christian opinion would support you.[35]

For avoidance of doubt Ramsey later clarified in correspondence exactly what he had said. It was:

"If Rhodesia goes over the brink I agree that it is not for us as Christian Churches to give the government military advice as to what is practicable or possible. That is not our function. But if the British Government thought it practicable to use force for the protection of the rights of the majority of the Rhodesian people, then I think that as Christians it will be right to use force to that end."[36]

The telegram to the Prime Minister and these words created a major row. There were a number of letters, such as the one from Joost de Blank, the former Archbishop of Cape Town, which simply said "Of course what you said was absolutely right" and others which lauded his courage. But the majority were vitriolic in their rage. The right wing, and in particular the Christian right wing, unleashed its sanctimonious, abusive hostility.

Ramsey was interviewed on the 10 o'clock programme of the Home service on 27 October, and again he tried to make his point clear.

"I've emphasized the fact – and so did the British Council of Churches emphasise the fact that it is for the Prime Minister and the government to make judgements as to what is really going to be practicable. And what we said was that if in the

163

judgement of the statesmen, it's really practicable to use force
in this context, then we believe the Christian conscience should
allow the use of force, if it's of the nature of the police force
in order to forestall and prevent more indiscriminate kinds of
force and violence".[37]

What Ramsey said was not platitudinous. Nor on the other
hand was he advocating a particular policy. He made it quite
clear that the decision was the responsibility of the Government.
Nevertheless, he offered clear guidance about the moral
dimension of this course of action, if the Government decided
on it. That is not the only model of how to speak for God in a
secular society, but it is one which does try to recognize the
respective responsibilities of government and church.

On the whole the Church of England tries to be fair and
representative of its different traditions in its leadership.
So it was not surprising that the Catholic Michael Ramsey
should have been succeeded by Donald Coggan, (Archbishop
of Canterbury from 1974–1980) a scholarly evangelical who
was Archbishop of York at the time. My main connection with
Donald Coggan was rather after this in my role as Chairman
of the Council of Christians and Jews, which I was for nine
years. The Archbishops are always joint Presidents of the
Council, together with the Chief Rabbi and other Christian and
Jewish leaders. Donald Coggan was an Old Testament Scholar
who always had a keen respect for Judaism but the shift in his
understanding of Christianity's relationship with Judaism in
his later years was quite remarkable.

In a 1985 lecture at St Paul's Cathedral, after listing five
attitudes which a Christian might bring to an encounter with
a Jewish friend, he ended up by saying that for a Christian to
share his or her faith is natural but this should be very much in
the form of a sensitive, gentle invitation. However, in 1992, in a
sermon at St Paul's Cathedral to celebrate the 50th anniversary
of the Council of Christians and Jews, he said that Judaism and

Christianity have so much in common which is essential for the very life of the world that "we should regard it as the truth of which we are common trustees and together we should make its light shine. We have a common message and, I would dare to say, a common mission".

In a third address on the theme, the annual Sacks lectures in 1995 at the University of Essex, Donald Coggan was even more explicit.

> I see two hands, grasped in a common task with Christian saying to Jew and Jew replying to Christian: "We have passed from hatred to tolerance, from tolerance to dialogue. Now, together, we go – in obedience to a common mission – to fulfil a shared task given to us by God. We are partners. We are co-trustees. Come, let us go – and go together."

This was a truly remarkable pilgrimage on the part of one of the most revered evangelical leaders of the last 50 years. When he was Archbishop of Canterbury, Dr George Carey, preaching the inaugural Donald Coggan lecture at the National Cathedral in Washington DC in April 2001, whilst deeply respecting his predecessor's learning and attitude, questioned that final step. Dr Carey argued against what seems to have become orthodoxy in the Episcopal Church in the United States, that there are two covenants one for Jews and one for Christians and that Christians should not try to convert Jews. He also questions Coggan's understanding of St Paul's teaching in Romans 9 to 11 which asks Christians to regard Judaism as valid in its own right without needing any fulfilment or consummation in Christianity. In a sensitive manner, that is based on the powerlessness of Christ's cross, he believes that Christians have a continuing duty to invite Jews to follow Christ. This should be on the basis of equality, with Christians being willing to learn from Jews and in the context of friendship when in most instances it would be the Jewish friend who would take the initiative in wanting to know something about Christianity. Nevertheless, "I do not abandon that desire to introduce them to my faith and the way I see it."

This lecture could have made for a major row in Great Britain because it was reported without any of the original subtleties and qualifications and Archbishop Carey could have been attacked for engaging in old-fashioned conversion of the Jews. However, the Chief Rabbi, in a great act of statesmanship, asked Rabbis of the United Synagogue, of which he is head, not to comment publicly on the Archbishop's lecture and they didn't. He also remarked that he understood that it was necessary for the Archbishop to say what he said and it was necessary for he himself to hear it. All this is an indication of how much has been achieved between the two communities, and between the Chief Rabbi and the then Archbishop of Canterbury in particular, in the way of mutual respect and supportive friendship. But my main point here is the remarkable re-think undertaken by Donald Coggan, in his understanding of the relationship between Judaism and Christianity.[38]

Bob Runcie (Archbishop of Canterbury 1980–1991) was Principal of Cuddesdon when I was a student there from 1961–3. The previous Principal, Edward Knapp Fisher, was an austere man who maintained that tradition in the college. As mentioned earlier, one of the features of the discipline of the college at the time was the banishing of women from anywhere near the college, even for married students. Bob Runcie decided to lighten this a little. I benefited from this new slightly more relaxed regime and because the college was very full when I applied late, I was billeted out to the house of a local farming family, the Palmers, who were sweetness itself and who allowed Jo my then fiancée to come and stay in the house on some weekends. Bob Runcie remained very fond of Jo all his ministry and always enquired most tenderly and genuinely after her.

Again, as mentioned earlier, as Principal, Bob Runcie was always very conscious of the great weight of the Cuddesdon past and those who guarded the tradition watchfully, as a result of which he was very careful about making any changes. It was probably true that he and all of us should have been more alert to the seismic changes which were beginning to take place in the wider culture at the time, but the Cuddesdon emphasis on the formation of a disciplined life of prayer and worship grounded us well for what lay ahead.

A highlight of any student's time there were the Principal's Pastoralia lectures, delivered in the final term before ordination. As the vast majority of students only wanted to get on as quickly as possible with the job of parish ministry these were eagerly devoured and Runcie's were superb. Also much admired were his introductions to visiting speakers, particularly the ones we had one night a week after dinner. In a few concise, amusing and illuminating sentences he was able to set a person and their subject before us. This did not come without cost. If you went to the cloakroom before one of these lectures you were likely to find the Principal pacing the corridor carefully working the sentences into shape in his head.

Bob Runcie kept in touch from time to time, for example, he wrote wonderfully supportive letters in his own hand for my ordination first as a deacon and then as a priest. But the next time I really saw him in action was when I was Dean of King's College, London, of which he was Visitor. I vividly remember one of his visits when I went round the great hall introducing him to members of staff. He showed then his extraordinary ability to instinctively hone in on someone's interests and through that to them as a person. Of course he had no difficulty doing this with the academics particularly with those from the arts departments. But he showed just the same ability with non-academics. For example, he found out that one lady, a non-academic, came from Liverpool, so could immediately mention the fact that his mother was a hairdresser in Liverpool. Although, as a result of his wartime experience as an officer in the Scots Guards he was a good friend with plenty of top-drawer people like Willie Whitelaw, he was not a snob and had no pretentions. This did not stop him having a thoroughly worldly understanding of where people stood in in the eyes of the world. So, at Cuddesdon before introducing me to someone he might whisper in my ear "farms 20,000 acres in Perthshire" or something similar. All that taken into account, he was wonderfully simpatico with everyone he met, whatever their background.

It was whilst I was at King's that from time to time he would ring up and ask me to write the draft of a sermon or speech for him. Of course one was very flattered and delighted to do this. But having done it he might not use a word, having perhaps asked others also to write something for him. It was very variable. I wrote what I thought was a profound sermon for a special anniversary of the BBC of which he used not a word. On the other hand, I wrote an article for *The Times* which appeared under his name, arguing that our defence of the Falklands satisfied Just War criteria, which appeared without a word being changed. I believe this way of using the help of others was a mistake.[39] It would have been better if he had thought out the main lines of what he wanted to say first before asking someone to write a script along those lines. He did not find the relentless pressure to produce things to say on public occasions at all easy, partly because he set himself high standards and knew how easy it was to fall below them. When on the phone about some script or other, he might sigh and say, "Many hurdles to jump before this one."

Nor did Runcie find the job itself easy, not least the press coverage. American bishops when they came over for the Lambeth conference were amazed at the way the press treated him. "It's a rough, tough world over here," I had to say to them.

In addition to the worries connected with the abduction of Terry Waite, the storm over photos of his wife, Lindy, in the papers and so on, he was unflagging in making himself available to other people. When I was with him in Singapore for a meeting of the Anglican Consultative Council, he was endlessly patient in talking to people and having his photo taken with them. I almost had to frog march him away to have a very occasional relaxing swim in a pool.

I was consecrated as Bishop of Oxford on Ascension Day 1987 in St Paul's Cathedral. It was a most wonderful and happy occasion. A friend, the composer Patrick Gowers, wrote a special anthem for it, *Viri Galilaei* which although a very ambitious piece for two organs is now often sung on Ascension Day in Cathedrals. Eric James preached a wonderful sermon, on the theme of E.M. Forster's words "Only Connect", particularly stressing my need to connect mind and heart. Then when the consecration was over, Bob Runcie literally seemed to dance up the aisle, holding my hand, as we made our way to the Great West Door. His funeral, in St Alban's Abbey was, in another way, an equally memorable event, attended as it was by so many of his friends. Especially moving was the lament as his body was piped out of the door to the grave in the grounds. With his passing, there was, for some of us a sense of Ichabod. Whatever future historians make of Bob Runcie's leadership as Archbishop, he was a great human being, with a very strong pastoral heart, often showing great care for ordinary individuals who were sick or in trouble, even in the midst of his heavy duties. For me he had an honour especially worth having, a Military Cross for bravery, which of course he never mentioned, indeed he was extremely reluctant to speak about himself at all.

When I became Bishop of Oxford in 1987, Bob Hardy, then Bishop of Lincoln, and I got together to form an episcopal cell for the mutual support of its members. We wanted this to represent every tradition in the Church of England, as well as being representative geographically. Amongst those invited to be a founding member was George Carey, who after making his reputation as an outstanding Principal of Trinity College, Bristol, was newly appointed as Bishop of Bath and Wells. This episcopal cell became an important part of all our lives, particularly in the early stages when most of us were new to the job and anxious to learn from one another. We met twice a year for 24 hours a time, revolving the venue around the different houses of our members. Wives would sometimes join us for a final meal together at the end of the meeting. It was a very supportive and helpful group. During its existence George was appointed Archbishop of Canterbury which he was from 1991–2002. I think he found it of particular help at that time sounding us out on his new heavy responsibilities. As is well known George comes from a humble background and left school at 16, getting an education, including a doctorate, later. He has a good brain, is a quick learner and is well organised. So at those meetings and in my other dealings with him over the years, you would invariably see him with a notebook and pen keeping notes of what was going on. You might also find him reading a book of New Testament scholarship in French on the plane. He was often prescient in his judgements. I remember being very surprised and somewhat shocked at the height of the scandals around Prince Charles, Princess Diana and Camilla Parker Bowles when George predicted that if Charles married Camilla it would not be too long before the nation accepted her and was willing to have her as queen. So it has proved.

Working with George at meetings of the House of Bishops, the General Synod and the Lambeth conference, he showed himself to be a strong leader, with clear ideas as to the reforms which were necessary and a determination to carry them out. This was particularly apparent after the financial losses incurred by the Church Commissioners shortly before he took over, when he brought about a major reorganisation in the structures of the

Church of England. All this of course was to make the church more effective in proclaiming Christ about which he cared deeply.

Apparently in Lambeth, George and his wife, Eileen, were sometimes referred to as William and Mary. If they were aware of this, I hope they took it as a compliment because they did indeed work as a team, and this was a great strength. Bishops' wives like clergy wives generally play very varied roles and there is no blueprint. Bob Runcie's wife, Lindy, had her much loved life as a music teacher and having been brought up very much free-range, remained a strong independent spirit. George and Eileen saw the ministry as very much a partnership, and George was not willing to see this in any other way. As already mentioned, I saw this attitude at first hand when I went with him on a visit to Russia, Armenia and Georgia when he insisted that she should be placed in a front car. At the Lambeth Conference, when Eileen presided over the simultaneous conference for wives, she showed herself very relaxed and at ease with herself on the public platforms introducing events. George and I did not agree on the issue of same-sex relationships, he taking a very conservative view, but I recognised and respected his role as a strong leader who tried to make the church better equipped to proclaim the faith in the face of all the difficulties, not least a cynical media. George and Eileen told each other that whatever the difficulties of the job they were going to enjoy it. That seemed to me rather a healthy attitude and one in marked contrast to both his predecessor and successor. Sadly, since his retirement, George has had a difficult time over his handling of the late Peter Ball, the Bishop of Gloucester for child abuse. Peter Ball was a darling of the establishment, including Prince Charles, all of whom protested his innocence. It put George in a very difficult position.

I was at a New Year's Day party given by Tony and Nancy Kenny on New Year's Day 2003 at which many of the intellectual

glitterati of Oxford were present. A few days earlier the Richard
Dimbleby lecture had been given on television by the newly
appointed Archbishop of Canterbury, Rowan Williams. It was
based on a major new book by the American scholar Philip
Bobbitt *The Shield of Achilles: war, peace and the course of history.*
Many of the guests, who were not inclined to be impressed by
clergymen, had stayed up late to watch it, and were impressed.
When sometime later I mentioned this to Philip Bobbitt,
he said to me that Rowan Williams was the one person who
really understood what the book was about. And that is just
one subject, not usually a major one for theologians. The range
of Rowan's intellectual interests is phenomenal as is the depth
of learning he shows in them. He has translated the Spanish
mystics and written about them, including what may well
become a classic of spirituality. He translates from the Russian
and in a short sabbatical when Archbishop, he wrote a major
book on Dostoevsky. He has written a major scholarly work on
Arius and published a multitude of brilliant essays on a range
of public policy issues. At the Hay literary festival one year,
when one of my books was shortlisted, Rowan was awarding the
prize. His summary of each of the four books and evaluation of
them was masterly. Later the same day he did a public dialogue
with Simon Russell Beale on Shakespeare and showed himself
to be deeply knowledgeable and full of insight on his work. And
this is only a portion of the subjects that Rowan has lectured and
written on, as well as being a respected poet himself. All this is
made possible first of all by the fact that he has a photographic
memory, and is able to look at a page of Latin or Greek and
remember it. He also has a good ear, being very musical with a
fine voice, and he can translate from 11 languages.

I regard myself as having a wide range of intellectual interests
but I find not only that Rowan's is wider, but that anything I
think I know about he seems to know more, in greater depth.
He appears to have read everything, remembered everything

and is able to talk or write with a magisterial authority that can only come from having fully assimilated the material and connected it to other areas of learning. He makes most so called public intellectuals seem very thin by comparison. In Sonnet 29, Shakespeare writes about "desiring this man's art and that man's scope". In his poem *Ash Wednesday,* Eliot has his own variation of this with the words "Desiring this man's gift and that man's scope". Some of us might be excused for desiring at least some of Rowan's gift and scope. I once teased Rowan and said to him, "God has given you every possible gift under the sun and as your punishment he has made you Archbishop of Canterbury."

In addition to these phenomenal intellectual gifts Rowan is a man of serious prayer and humility, deeply caring and committed to the most vulnerable. This is the Rowan that emerges so wonderfully when he is preaching at the Eucharist, especially in an informal setting. Those who experience this always regard it as a privilege. Yet he also has a reputation for being unnecessarily difficult and obscure. The *New Statesman,* for which he is now a lead reviewer, recently printed some letters from readers complaining that Rowan's reviews were too difficult. He can indeed be a very difficult writer. This is partly, I think, because he cannot formulate a thought in his mind without at the same time being aware of all the qualifications and nuances that are necessary. The result is that it is not always easy to sum up what he has said in one's own words. It is also because his range of reference is always so wide. Then there is his clear dislike of anything approaching a cliché or saying the obvious. I have written in an earlier chapter about my nomination of Jeffrey John as Bishop of Reading and how Rowan withdrew his initial acceptance of this, so I will not repeat it here.

I did not know Rowan in the early years of his ministry but was always aware of his reputation as a brilliant scholar and holy priest. Again, although he was Lady Margaret Professor of Divinity in Oxford for some of the time I was Bishop, I did not know him well then, though I did chair a Church of England working party of which he was a member which produced a worthwhile report.[40] It was when he became Archbishop for the last four years of my time as Bishop of Oxford that I worked most closely with him. He was totally at ease chairing the House of Bishops meetings, clearly mastering the paperwork without undue angst. The most remarkable meeting was at one of the heights of controversy over same-sex relationships. When the formal business was over, he simply sat on a chair facing us and opened up his heart as well as his mind over what was happening. He spoke with characteristic eloquence for nearly an hour. I sat next to Tom Wright, then Bishop of Durham, who in fact took a much more conservative position than did Rowan. I noticed that Tom was in tears. But we were all equally moved.

I have been hugely influenced by Rowan, first all of by his example of holiness and humility and then in almost every area of intellectual endeavour that we have both thought about. On the central Christian beliefs, I have been much reassured and strengthened in a Trinitarian view of God by Rowan's continued emphasis on this in everything he writes. I remember reading two books on the Trinity some fifty years ago and thinking how naturally and essentially my own Christian thinking was Trinitarian and so much of what Rowan writes resonates and reinforces this. But he has shifted my thinking in many areas, including his emphasis on God creating a new humanity round Jesus, and following on from this the essential nature of the church as the embodiment of this.

Justin Welby, who was installed as Archbishop of Canterbury in 2013 came from a career on the financial side of the oil industry. This has given him a grasp of the way the secular world works and some authority when he speaks about financial matters. His earlier work in the church, when he made numerous visits to conflict areas in Nigeria to try to bring about reconciliation, also indicated a willingness to be bold. As mentioned earlier, this was quickly shown when he spoke out against pay day lenders like Wonga, saying that the church would put them out of business by supporting and forming credit unions. But when it was later shown that the Church of England had invested in an equity fund that had shares in Wonga, it was to be typical of him that he quickly admitted that this, which was unknown to him and the church's ethical investment advisory group, was highly embarrassing. Unlike so many public spokespeople who appear on the media he does not equivocate but gives a clear, honest answer. Indeed, one of his most endearing features is his complete lack of side and his self-deprecating sense of humour. Shortly after his appointment was announced, I met Giles Fraser who had just interviewed him. On a number of issues they would not agree but Giles was totally bowled over, "'e does human" he kept repeating in his best mockney. That is certainly my experience of Justin both in private and on public occasions. It goes a long way to disarming any instinct to carp and criticise. This is one of the features that enables him to be at ease in his contributions in the House of Lords. This is no doubt also helped by the fact that he comes from a social background unlikely to be intimidated by its membership, which also included, before he died, his stepfather, Charles Williams.

His interventions on pay day lending, banking (he is a member of the banking commission) and other financial issues, means that he has achieved a rare miracle. He got the national press talking about the Church of England and money rather than the Church of England and gay sex. The other miracle was the way that after the final push to get women bishops floundered under Archbishop Rowan, Justin started again and in a remarkably short time brought it about. The Vatican require three miracles for sainthood, so we only need one more. The fact that he was able to bring this about was no doubt due in part to the sense of shock and sombre reckoning that fell on the church after the previous failure but also significantly to Justin's capacity to break down barriers and his experience in reconciliation work.

Justin Welby has been criticised in some quarters on two counts. One is that he is bringing in a more managerial style, particularly when it comes to training up new leaders for the church, and secondly for relying too much on his personal relationships rather than the structures of the church. In relation to the latter, the two approaches are surely not mutually exclusive and the creation of good relationships at the top are what can help achieve institutional rapprochement.[41]

A feature of spiritual maturity in the leadership of the Church of England is a person's capacity to genuinely enter into some of the riches of traditions other than their own. This was true of George Carey as he came to appreciate and make his own some Catholic practices. It was true of Rowan Williams in his positive words about the charismatic movement. This capacity is even more pronounced in Justin Welby. Converted within and nourished in the milieu of Holy Trinity, Brompton, he is able to speak very naturally about his experience there. When asked if he spoke in tongues he replied, "Oh yes, it's just a routine part of spiritual discipline – you choose to speak and you speak a language that you don't know. It just comes." At the same time he uses Catholic spiritual disciplines in his personal prayer, has a Roman Catholic spiritual director and has formed a religious community at Lambeth Palace.

Justin Welby has a clear sense of what is needed in a leader. When a new Archbishop takes up his post he is likely to find his diary committed for months if not years ahead as all the different departments book in time for different aspects of the job. The first thing Justine did was to clear his diary for the next six months. He wanted to set his own priorities. Some have felt that his leadership during the first phase of the COVID-19 crisis was missing. He spent a fair amount of time then simply working as a hospital chaplain.

These seven archbishops have all been very different people, as have the gifts they have brought to the role of Archbishop and the style of leaderships they have adopted. But all have been gifted and godly men (and until now, of course, they have all been men) through whom God has enriched the Church of England in fresh ways. All have touched, and in some ways influenced, my life.[42]

In procession in Oxford, with Rowan Williams,
the Archbishop of Canterbury.

Chapter 21

Apologetics

I once heard Donald Mackinnon, whom I described earlier as the big influence on my thinking when I was at Cambridge, say that "apologetics is the lowest form of Christian life". I know what he means. It is ghastly when someone argues in favour of Christianity in the style of politicians justifying a political policy, focussing on the opposition's weak points and ignoring their own weaknesses. Christian apologetics should be a world away from any kind of propaganda or spin doctoring. For in the end, and this was MacKinnon's passion, Christians are in the truth business and that may mean facing very uncomfortable truths.

We should not draw the wrong conclusion from this, however, and assume there is some kind of neutral standpoint on the world. There is not. The fact that a Christian will describe the world from the standpoint of their faith is no more or less problematic than an agnostic or atheist doing so. None of them are speaking from a neutral realm, all bring some basic assumptions and values to bear. What distinguishes legitimate apologetics from forms of propaganda or spin doctoring, however, is a willingness to focus on the strongest arguments against its own position, not the weakest, and a willingness to recognise truth wherever it comes from.

In Christian history, apologetics is associated first of all with a group of Christian thinkers in the second century who sought to relate the Christian faith to the surrounding Greek philosophical culture. In every age there have been those like them who have sought to relate the faith to the culture and questions of the time, as I have, but I have always borne in mind the warning of MacKinnon that it is the lowest form of

Christian life. Nevertheless, I believe that anyone who tries to communicate a Christian view of life today needs to be an apologist, in the sense that they need to take seriously the questions and objections of the prevailing world view, which in our time is secularism. Indeed, if they do not do this it is difficult to see how they can communicate anything meaningful at all. So I come back to the title of that MacKinnon inaugural lecture "The Borderlands of Theology". Thinking and speaking as a Christian today means living on the border and feeling the incursions from outside. The word apologetics is not a very happy one in so far as it brings to mind the word apology. Apologists are certainly not apologising for the faith, though they may very well need to apologise for a great deal of Christian practice. Nor is the phrase "defence of the faith" entirely happy. For me apologetics is about trying to recognise where God is present in the culture and questions of our time.

Christian apologetics might also involve putting forward arguments in favour of what is believed to be an orthodox rather than a heterodox version of the faith, so it may have to operate on two fronts. I wrote a book setting out my basic understanding of the faith and its practical outworking in personal life in 1981, clearly drawing on my time at Fulham leading adult confirmation classes and other study groups.[43] A more obvious work of apologetics was one that followed a few years later on the Resurrection of Christ.[44] Always a controversial subject from its early preaching in Jerusalem and Athens, it was in the news in the 1980s because of misinterpreted words of the then Bishop of Durham, Dr David Jenkins. One Easter Sunday he had emphasised from the pulpit that the resurrection of Jesus should not be seen as a conjuring trick with bones. But he was reported as saying just the opposite, namely that it was a conjuring trick with bones. I vividly remember a conversation I had at the time with a friend who was a businessman. "It's all very well the Bishop not believing in the resurrection, Richard, but when it comes to supporting the miners!"

The resurrection of Christ is not to be understood like a Stanley Spencer painting in which people clamber out of their tombs. But nor is it just an inner experience. The tomb was found empty and a good number of people claimed to have encountered an objective presence and as a result were seized with the conviction that this was the beginning of a new creation. The Resurrection of Christ was like no other human happening and is comparable only with creation *ex nihilo* in the beginning and the transfiguring of all existence at the end of time. Moreover, this presence was like none other. It was an appearance from heaven, as it were, not a body, however transformed, climbing out of the tomb but an appearance of the risen Christ from the heart of God. How can we best understand and describe it, especially when the stories of the encounters are clearly written up from particular theological perspectives? My own answer differs from that of many if not most, but I hold firmly to the view that we are dealing with something "objective" and real, not just a projection of the human imagination.

Another major controversy then and later was the "sea of faith" school, taking its title from the famous poem by Matthew Arnold "On Dover Beach" with its lines:

The Sea of Faith
Was once, too, at the full, and round earth's shore
Lay like the folds of a bright girdle furled.
But now I only hear
Its melancholy, long, withdrawing roar,

In place of traditional faith in the reality of God, adherents of this school adopted a kind of Buddhism in which religious practices were valued while any kind of claim about ultimate reality was dropped. I came into this controversy as a result of a book by a clergyman who held this view to which I wrote a response arguing for a symbolic realism.[45] Some people were arguing that a priest with such views ought to resign their orders or have their licence taken away. But it seemed to me much better to refute the arguments in question. Of course all religious language is symbolic or metaphorical, and everything we say about God however true is also limited, partial and misleading. A failure to understand the nature of religious language is at the heart of so many unhelpful controversies. Those of us with a responsibility to teach the faith should be explaining this more often. At the same time real claims are being made.

Apologetics takes a number of different forms depending on the area of knowledge that it seeks to relate to and there have been some excellent Christian thinkers in the realms of science, like Alister McGrath, and in the field of philosophy, like Keith Ward. Because of my role as Bishop of Oxford and the notorious debate between one of my predecessors and Thomas Huxley, I got drawn into the science and evolution debate and did my little bit in debates against Richard Dawkins and others of that ilk.[46] I remember one such debate on an anniversary of the Wilberforce Huxley debate when I had to debate with Richard Dawkins in the wonderful surroundings of the Museum of Natural History in Oxford. I felt it got off to a great start when we opened with a full orchestral rendering of Hayden's Creation with its theme of the heavens telling the glory of God! But I never got seriously into this area, first because of far better qualified people than myself already doing it, and secondly because I actually think it is a distraction from the more pressing intellectual issues with which people of faith ought to be grappling. I have sometimes teased Richard Dawkins by saying, "There are enough good reasons against religion, Richard, without dragging science into it."

The first decade of the twenty-first century was dominated in the religious sphere by the so called new atheists. Although this brought forth some powerful intellectual responses from a number of Christian thinkers it was not a debate that attracted me. First, because these atheist writers, who were on the whole not philosophers had a very simplistic understanding of the relationship of science and religion, and secondly because they deliberately focussed on American fundamentalism as the form of Christianity to refute. They did not attempt to grapple with serious and subtle Christian thinkers who were not fundamentalists. My complaint then was that there were no serious atheists around, comparable to Marghanita Laski of a previous generation who had a series of high level public debates of great integrity with Metropolitan Anthony Bloom. So one piece I wrote later argued for the desperate importance of taking serious atheism seriously and lamenting the fact that there were no serious atheists around.[47] I have debated a few times with A.C. Grayling who likes to put on a not very convincing Irish accent and talk about fairies at the bottom of the garden. The fact is that the most sophisticated minds for most of history have believed in God and to reduce the argument to this level is childish. The arguments of serious atheism must be listened to but it has very little to do with either the science/ religion debate or philosophy as such, except to show that so called arguments leave the question of God's reality open. This can neither be proved nor disproved, and from a theological point of view the attempt to prove it is misguided, for God is by definition a reality that makes a total difference to our lives not the conclusion of a piece of logic. The reason Darwin lost his faith, though he probably never lost it completely, was first because evolution clearly contradicted the simplistic view of the Bible with which he had been brought up, and secondly, even more crucially, the tragic death of his daughter. His experience would be replicated by very many more. And that's where I feel

Christian apologetics needs to focus, on the evil and suffering in the world. But there are other areas as well which I have sought to address.

A sentence by Alec Vidler in his history of the church in the nineteenth century has pursued and prodded me all my life. There he wrote that the great Victorian agnostics who turned away from the church did so not because of the rise of science or the advent of biblical criticism but because what the church called upon them to believe with a sense of its moral superiority struck them as morally inferior to their own highest beliefs and standards.[48] The church still fails to take this seriously by continuing to claim the high moral ground and failing to realise that its critics claim the same ground. This was the theme of a book I wrote in 2002. Then as now there was a large body of people who called themselves spiritual, rather than religious, and they objected to religion on moral grounds as much as anything else. I tried to take those moral arguments seriously as indicated by the chapter headings, The Despot God, The Male Boss, Eternal punishment, The Oddness of praise, Does God have Favourites?, Religion keeps people immature, Christianity bangs on about sin and guilt, Christians eat God, Christianity is just for wimps, and so on.[49] These are the kinds of questions lurking around in people's subconscious whether or not they are always articulated. They have to be faced and addressed. Too often old themes are preached without any awareness that there are some fundamentally different assumptions in our culture, which we breathe in whether we like it or not. For example, what is the point of the church talking about self-denial if the leading idea in our culture is the importance of self-fulfilment? It is not a question of jettisoning the idea of self-denial, far from it, but of getting people to ask questions about the nature of the self and how fulfilment is in fact to be found. Here I have found a rather surprising person, D.H. Lawrence, helpful, for Lawrence had a sure feel for what Christian virtues were really about and also how they have been distorted. For example, in his short poems about humility, one of them reads:

> To be humble before other men is degrading. I am humble
> before no man
> And I want no man to be humble before me.
> But when I see the life-spirit fluttering and struggling in a man
> I want to show always the human, tender reverence.[50]

The best known Christian apologist in the last half of the twentieth century was C.S. Lewis and his books still sell in the millions. Lewis was by nature pugnacious, a pugnacity which was honed by the argumentative style of Oxford tutorials. His style was to expose and demolish the weakness in the arguments of his opponents in a way which conceded little if anything. In fact, however, his real strength lay elsewhere. As Austin Farrer put it:

> His real power was not proof, it was depiction. There lived
> in his writings a Christian universe which could be both
> thought and felt, in which he was at home, and in which he
> made his readers feel at home. Belief is natural, for the world
> is so. It is enough to let it be seen so.[51]

So it is that his best writings are his war time essays like "The Weight of Glory", his Narnia series, especially *The Lion, the Witch and the Wardrobe,* and his later writings when he wrestles with issues like prayer and his own grief on the death of his wife. In these writings the argumentative element is less to the fore and his deep learning and creative imagination were put at the service of showing what the world looks like from a Christian point of view.[52]

This brings to the fore another sentence by Austin Farrer which has always been fundamental to my approach. In one sermon he compares the simple faith of his mother with someone who might have a more wide ranging intelligence and then continues:

> The centre of your Christian conviction, whatever you may think, will be where my mother's was... in your exploration of grace, in your walking with God. But faith perishes if it is walled in or confined. If it is anywhere it must be everywhere, like God himself: if God is in your life he is in all things, for he is God. You must be able to spread the area of recognition for him, and the basis of your conviction about him, as widely as your thought may range.[53]

I have sought to spread the area of recognition about God not only in relation to the assumptions and arguments of our predominantly secular culture but to four areas in particular, the aesthetic dimension, the moral dimension, the political realm and the existence of other religions. This means that I have not only been interested in particular issues in these areas but foundational questions connected with them and their relation to the Christian faith.

Like almost all other human beings I am moved by the experience of beauty in nature, whether it is the mountains, the coast, woods or a single blossom. I also respond to the arts, particularly the visual arts. As mentioned earlier this interest began during long vacations from Cambridge when a group of us toured the continent in an old car spending our days in museums and art galleries. Since then my wife and I have been fortunate enough to spend many holidays doing just that. In addition there has been the huge bonus of lecturing on Swan Hellenic Cruises for nearly 30 years enabling me to explore the art and culture of many countries but particularly the art of Europe and the Mediterranean.

Beauty is an unfashionable word in artistic circles today, where the drive is all to produce something new and this often means something that will shock. But a work can only be a work of art if it has some aesthetic quality, and that means some sense of symmetry or balance, elegance or form, as well as vitality. These are just the qualities that ancient writers regarded as fundamental to any experience of beauty and which I believe still draw us in the visual arts both in ancient art and in some modern works as well. So the question from an apologetics point of view is how can we see the footprint of God here? This is particularly important today when the arts, particularly music, have come to occupy the place in many people's lives that once was occupied by religion.

Ancient Christian thinkers took it for granted that this dimension of beauty, like the quest for truth and goodness was integral to faith because for so much of Christian history, both Western and Eastern, the faith has walked hand in hand with some form of Platonism. For Platonism the trio of beauty, truth and goodness are the fundamental categories of a transcendent realm. So it was, for example, that St Augustine finds it quite natural to pray to God as "Thou beauty most ancient and withal so fresh". Sadly, this theological appreciation of beauty began to slip away from Christian thought at the Reformation and has been lost to many forms of Protestantism, sometimes even being seen as a hostile alternative to a biblical view of the world. But as the great Roman Catholic theologian Hans Urs von Balthazar put it about beauty: "We can be sure that whoever sneers at her name as if she were an ornament of a bourgeois past – whether he admits it or not – can no longer pray and soon will be no longer able to love."[54]

We can easily see the link between beauty and God when we remember that the only reason for faith is that we have come to see that God is good, all good, our true and everlasting good. It is this intrinsic goodness which draws and attracts us and invites a response. In a similar way, beauty draws and attracts us, indeed, more than that it can tantalises us with a sense of wanting to pass into it. Apologetics in the sense that Farrer would define it, spreading the area of our recognition for God as widely as it will range, seeks to understand how these two dimensions of human experience relate to one another. This is what I sought to do in my book *Art and the Beauty of God: a Christian understanding.*[55] This was chosen as his book of the year for 1993 by Anthony Burgess in *The Observer*.

My other writing in this area was not so obviously theological but was based on the recognition that many people in our age are drawn to the visual rather than verbal. So I wrote *A Gallery of Reflections. the Nativity of Christ: Devotional reflections on the Christmas story in Art.*[56] This has about 40 fine reproductions of paintings on the Christmas story. It was followed by *The Passion in Art*, a history of the different ways the cross has been depicted in Christian history which tried to bring out the different theological understandings involved.[57] Because of my long standing love of icons, and experience of extensive travelling in which I was able to see the frescoes and mosaics of the Orthodox churches, I was able in these books to bring together not only ancient and modern depictions but Western and Eastern ones as well. Ashgate published this book as they did *The Image of Christ in Modern Art.*[58] This was written to challenge the widespread assumption that modern art, which I take to be with the birth of modernism about 1913, has neglected Christian themes. I believed that there was much more art which was related to traditional Christian images than was usually allowed, not least in our own time. It was my most seriously academic book in this field, pioneering new ground, but one which has also had popular appeal. Since then I have written *Seeing God in God: the Christian faith in 30 images.*[59] Drawing on images from Eastern Christianity as well as Western, ancient and modern, it seeks to offer a fresh accessible way into the faith while at the same time facing the most fundamental questions.

The second area in which I have sought to spread the area of my recognition is that of ethics and values. I had taught and written on specific areas such as war and medical ethics but what I sought to do here was to consider some foundational questions. For example, how do we relate what we understand to be God's will to the ordinary set of moral values and ethical principle but which the non-religious live?

If everyone, by virtue of their humanity has some capacity to make moral choices what if anything does a Christian view add to this; what difference does it make? These questions were addressed in *The Re-enchantment of Morality*.[60] In addition to laying out what a Christian ethic looks like in relation to other ethical approaches it sought to show how this worked out in relation to the great drivers of human behaviour, sex, money, power and fame. The book was short listed for the 2011 Michael Ramsey prize. On the first evening at the Hay Festival, where the prize was to be announced, we were sitting down for supper when one of the judges, Simon Russell Beale, made a point of coming over to talk to me and tell me how very much he had enjoyed and appreciated the book. I knew from that moment I had not won!

The third area in which I have tried to spread the area of recognition and relate to modern questioning is the political realm. Here again my concern was not so much with political policies but foundational questions about the values which should guide our life together. This resulted in *Faith in Politics? Rediscovering the Christian roots of our political values*.[61] This set out to challenge the assumption that the values underpinning our political life are primarily secular. I sought to show that they are deeply rooted, not just historically but philosophically in the Christian faith. I looked at issues like democracy, human rights, and values like equality, liberty and human community. The title of the book has a question mark in it, not always noticed. It reflected a widespread loss of confidence in our political system and resentment towards its politicians. I wanted to show that our political institutions and the values they express are crucial for our life together. The book also argued, following the Harvard Professor Michael Sandel, that the ideology which now rules in our society, a combination of social and market liberalism, is disastrous. Free choice, however important, is only one of a set of values which is needed for human communities to flourish. These other values are not just personal preferences, they belong in the public shared realm.

The writing of these books was greatly helped by the fact that I was appointed Gresham Professor of Divinity from 2008–12. Gresham College, found by a City of London philanthropist in the seventeenth century has a number of professorships with wonderful titles like rhetoric and astronomy. The professors have to give six public lectures a year, which many of us did in a lecture room in the Museum of London. It was a particularly good venue for the use of PowerPoint, so I could show my images of paintings off to their full advantage. From these lectures also came, in due course, not only my books on art but *Haunted by Christ: modern writers and the struggle for faith.*[62] This reflects my life-long love of literature.

A book which draws together the thinking of my whole lifetime was published under the heading of *The Beauty and the Horror: searching for God in a suffering world.*[63] As the title indicates it addresses that what I earlier wrote was the most fundamental question of all. In this book I take with utter seriousness the strength of the case against my belief. As mentioned earlier, one of my tutors at Cambridge, Howard Root, likened the situation to that of a good detective in a clever crime novel. All the evidence seems to point in one direction but the good detective has noticed a clue which others have overlooked and which casts a totally different light on the whole story. So much of the evidence seems to point to the conclusion that there cannot be a wise and loving power behind the universe. But the Christian has noticed an overlooked clue in the person of Jesus Christ. There is a story about a Rabbi and a priest talking together and the rabbi saying, "Father, I believe in God, but I cannot believe in Jesus Christ," to which the priest responds, "If it was not for Jesus Christ I could not believe in God." My own faith is of a similar kind. I continue to go on in faith and hope and love in the faith that God himself has accepted the consequences of creating a world like this one by becoming part of the flux of history in Jesus in order to change it from within; that God has raised him to an eternal contemporaneity and that he has given us the promise that in the end his divine purpose of love will prevail over all evil, including death. Central to the book is the moral case against God as put by Ivan Karamazov in Dostoevsky's great novel. "It's not God I don't believe in, Alyosha, it's just that I return him my ticket."

What also has concerned me in a way that does not seem to trouble too many others is how we relate the all too real suffering of the cross to faith in the resurrection in a way that does not make the resurrection seem like a happy ending tacked on at the end, or which takes away from the horror of death by crucifixion. Can the resurrection of Christ be talked about in a way which is as real as the cross? Can we talk about an eternal life with God with the same kind of integrity we talk about the anguish of this life?[64] This issue was touched on in some of my earlier books and gets taken up again in *The Beauty and the Horror*. Here again it is a question of moral sensibility, rather than a strictly philosophical one that has concerned me; a mixture of emotion and aesthetic and moral judgement which makes people react against the Christian claim. It is this kind of moral feeling element that I have tried to take seriously and which has been central to my work as an apologist.

The fourth area in which I have tried to relate the Christian faith to the world and questions of today is in the field of Christianity and other religions and I write something about this in the next chapter.

Chapter 22

All God's Children

As a student at Cambridge I attended a course of lectures on the Christian attitude to other religions. The lecturer offered a sharp critique of a Barthian approach, which was very popular in some quarters at the time. Barth made a sharp contrast between religions in general, which he thought were man-made attempts to reach out to God, and Christian faith which was the result of his revelation in Jesus Christ, and a matter of pure grace. The lecturer denied that there was this great abyss between the two and argued for some commonality. I found myself much in sympathy with his approach and was influenced in particular by the work of the distinguished scholar R.C. Zaehner which took a similar position. My first real attempt to engage with another religion, however, was later in my ministry when I was at Fulham and I was asked to join the Manor House Group.

The Manor House Group was initiated by Rabbi Tony Bayfield of the Sternberg Centre in Finchley, the administrative centre of Reform Judaism. It consisted of about fifteen thoughtful Rabbis and priests in the London area. We met twice a year for most of a day and once a year when we went away for a weekend together at the Quaker Centre in Charney Bassett in Oxfordshire. The pattern was a very simple one. We selected a subject and heard two prepared papers on it, one from a Jew and one from a Christian, this was followed by discussion and lunch and further discussion. I think all the members of this group found it hugely influential in their thinking, certainly I did. What was interesting was the way cultural differences emerged alongside theological convergences. For example, when a Christian read a paper we all listened quietly until they had finished before initiating a general discussion. When a Rabbi read a paper he had hardly got out two sentences before one of the other rabbis would be disagreeing with some point! Lively discussion, including strong disagreement, was for some of them a culture they had breathed in from birth. Another cultural difference emerged on the annual walk we liked to take, or some of us did, on the Ridgeway. The Christians came prepared with boots or good walking shoes, the Rabbis tended to have black city shoes. All this added to the fun and merriment we shared along with the serious discussion. After some years in existence, we decided to draw this phase of the group to an end by producing a book with some of the fruit of our years together. This we did, with thirteen of us writing a chapter on different areas of the subject matter we had considered.[65] Out of this group came deep and lasting friendships, especially with Julia Neuberger and her family.

No doubt because of my increasing involvement with Judaism not only through this group but as a member of an Anglican Jewish symposium, and an international three faiths network under the active auspices of the Duke of Edinburgh, Prince Hassan of Jordan and Sir Evelyn Rothschild, I was asked to be Chair of the Council of Christians and Jews. I was nominated for this by the remarkable Sir Sigmund Sternberg, and had nine quite testing but rewarding years in this position. So many stereotypes still exist in the Christian mind about Judaism that the task of education has to be done afresh in every generation. Too often still Judaism is presented from the pulpit only as the foil for Christian faith with Judaism as the bad guy, legalistic, obsessed with minor detail, and Christianity as the good guy coming to the rescue. Too often still Christianity is presented as having replaced or superseded Judaism, indeed the very use of the term Old Testament, rather than the Hebrew Scriptures can convey this. CCJ exists not just to counter anti-Semitism, which has been growing in recent years, but to help both religions have a deeper respect for one another as valid in their own right. At one time during my chairmanship there was a move to turn it into a three faiths organisation. But though there was and is a need for three faith and multifaith organisations the Presidents of CCJ at the time, especially the Chief Rabbi and the Archbishop of Canterbury, argued that there was still a unique and important job to be done in relation to these two religions, tangled and painful as their history has been.

Another issue that aroused a great deal of feeling at this time in the Jewish Community was whether any Jewish leader other than the Chief Rabbi should be a President, for from the Christian side there are a number of different presidents, representing different denominations. But for many years there was no Reform or Liberal Jewish representation. Mainly due to the persistent pressure of Rabbi John Rayner this was eventually rectified.

The most contentious issue then as now was the question of Israel. The Churches have close links with the Churches in the Middle East and organisations like Christian Aid work in Palestinian areas, so understand their perspective, as of course do very many Jews. But CCJ was clear that whatever disagreements there might be with particular policies of particular Israeli governments, the right of the State of Israel to live in peace and security needed to be affirmed. In due course I published *After the Evil: Christianity and Judaism in the Shadow of the Holocaust,* a book which deals with a wide range of the issues which have troubled the relationship between the two religions and which have to be radically re-thought in the light of the Holocaust.[66]

I have always maintained that there are three simple but fundamental principles of interfaith dialogue. First, to let the dialogue partner speak for themselves and define themselves in their own way. For too much of the time we see the other through the spectacles provided by our own cultural or religious tradition. We define them in our own terms and project onto them a series of stereotypes. It is up to them to explain how they understand and see the world and up to us to listen and try to comprehend this viewpoint, not only intellectually but imaginatively as well.

Secondly, to try to identify and affirm any common ground that there might be. It would be very surprising indeed if none could be found, if not in belief at least in fundamental values.

Thirdly, to be honest about disagreements. Some people wrongly think that for interfaith dialogue to take place it is necessary for people to leave their most strongly held beliefs behind. That is totally false. For dialogue to be real, it must be possible to share disagreements, even on very fundamental issues. In my experience when an atmosphere of respect and trust has been built up, as happened with the Manor House Group, and some commonalities have been identified, disagreement is both possible and fruitful.

It was these three principles that I again brought to bear when as Bishop of Oxford I convened the Oxford Abrahamic Group, bringing together Jewish, Christian and Muslim Scholars for two days a year at Bishop's House. I had good links with the Oxford Centre for Islamic Studies and in addition Tim Winter, a very scholarly convert to Islam, used to travel over from Cambridge to join us. Our method was similar to that I had used with the Manor House Group. Before I left Oxford, we put together a book structured on the principles of dialogue that we had also used in our discussions over the years. A number of topics were taken, for example, the position of Abraham in the three religions or the attitude to women. A Jewish, Christian and Muslim Scholar each wrote a piece from the standpoint of their religion, then a final section in the area of study tried to identify what was held in common, where the disagreements lay and where further work would be useful.[67]

The membership of the Oxford Abrahamic Group included some very distinguished scholars, but it was more difficult than the Manor Hour Group to create continuity and therefore a community of study. This was quite simply that being situated in a university town, with people used to dropping in and out of seminars it was difficult to achieve the kind of stability of attendance that we had achieved in London. Nevertheless, I believe we achieved something worthwhile.

Some views make interfaith dialogue very difficult if not impossible. For example, if you believe that all other religions are totally false or evil it is hard to see how you can built up the mutual respect that is necessary for a genuine sharing. But I don't think that the other extreme, the view that all religions are really saying the same thing is very helpful either. The fact is that they are saying some quite different things. Buddhism in its classical form does not believe in a creator God, and Hinduism in its popular manifestation believes in many gods. Christianity believes that in Jesus there is a unique disclosure of the heart of God. Both Judaism and Islam deny this.

The best starting point, I believe, is an honest recognition that there are real differences. But together with this it is highly desirable to be able to find some theological space in one's own tradition which allows for other approaches. My own is the simple fact that God is the creator of all human beings and through his spirit touches the hearts of all in every culture. Through the process of dialogue, as outlined above, letting the other speak for themselves, I would hope to identify some common ground. I would also hope to have my own vision of God enlarged and enriched by what the other says to me. Perhaps my own understanding will also be corrected in some way. For although I am committed to the Christian faith, I do not believe my understanding of it is the last word. Rather, the God who is beyond anything I can grasp now is leading me into a fuller realisation of the truth, and interfaith dialogue is one of the ways in which this can happen. This is my experience of what has happened. I have come to a deeper understanding and respect for the position of the other, and my own faith has also been enlarged. Sometimes it is through dialogue with other religions that people are led to rediscover truths buried in their own.

More important than talking together is acting together. A memorable moment for me in Oxford occurred during one of the recurring crises in the Middle East. We had a peace march that started with prayers outside the synagogue and continued to the University church for more prayer there before finishing at the mosque with prayer and hospitality. Several hundred people went on this march, each with a white balloon floating above them.

My experience of dialogue has been with members of the Abrahamic religions not with those which originated on the Indian subcontinent, so I look to the books of my friend Keith Ward, who knows those religions well, for illumination on their points of congruity with Christian faith. But my starting point is well summed up in the words of Austin Farrer. "The sacraments are God's covenanted mercies. Of God's uncovenanted mercies there is no end." So I believe that God's grace touches people in many different ways under many forms. But from a more questioning point of view, I find it difficult to make any sense of the idea of a continuing self, moving at death from one life to another. Every life seems to me a unique product of its time and place and is called in that particularity to a relationship with God that endures beyond time in another dimension altogether. Also I do not believe with Buddhism that the main challenge in life is to achieve detachment from suffering. The main challenge is to alleviate the suffering of others and its reality remains the greatest intellectual obstacle to Christian faith.

In more recent years I have been a trustee of the Woolf Institute in Cambridge for the study of relations between Jews, Christians and Muslims under their able and dynamic director, Ed Kessler. This has pioneered new work, especially in relation to public and social policy, and it moved into a new purpose built centre in the grounds of Westminster College in 2017. The Woolf Institute initiated the Commission on *Religion and Belief in British Public Life* of which I was a member and which produced its influential report in 2016 and which is available on the internet. The commission had members representing all the major religious traditions and a number of articulate secular voices. The main tension that emerged was between those with a religious perspective who valued the Christian heritage and institutions of the country, and the secular view which wanted a strictly neutral public space. The non-Christian religions value the establishment of the Church of England, for example, because they believe it helps them make their own contribution to public life. This gets short shrift from secularists. And that is perhaps one of the intellectual divides in our country now on the issue of religion.

Chapter 23

The mystical communion of all faithful people

As I indicated in earlier chapters, before ordination I had no experience of the church as a Christian community. My journey of faith was essentially a private inner one not one inspired by a good experience of community. Attendance at school chapel could not count as that and chapel at university only partially so. At Cuddesdon, although the Principal laid great stress on the college as a community, I don't think it made much impact on me, no doubt my fault, partly because I was at the same time engaged to Jo who was living in London and she occupied a fair amount of my emotions. It was as a Curate in Hampstead and as Vicar of All Saints, Fulham, but especially by my time at Wells Theological College that the concept of Christian Community became more of a reality. From the point of view of theology, it is the writings of Rowan Williams that have made me see more forcefully than before that our relationship to Christ cannot be separated from the creation of a new humanity in and around him.

Like the vast majority of people who have any kind of living religion, when I emerged into the light of faith it was within the religious tradition of my culture, which happened to be Anglican, and I followed that way without too much agonising at first. It was familiar, yet it also allowed me to express the seriousness of my faith by taking a particular focus within it. It might have been as an Evangelical, but though I respect and often hugely admire particular evangelicals, there were aspects which repelled rather than drew me. The Catholic approach, however, left me free both to be drawn in more gradually, and also assert that I was indeed serious about my faith. It was with a sense of doing something beyond the run of the mill that I first started going to early services of Holy Communion mid-week. Then, later it was with a sense of daring as I started making the sign of the cross, and even going to confession.

As a Catholic minded Anglican, I had to consider, as did others in my position, whether the Church of England really was part of the Catholic church or whether I should become a Roman Catholic. This was an issue of great debate all through the nineteenth century and often reflected in its novels and it is still an issue today for some Christians. I continue to have enormous admiration for the Roman Catholic Church, for its internationalism and ethnic diversity and its capacity to produce and nurture so many great saints. As a person of tidy mind I also like the idea of an organisation that is clear in what it believes and teaches. The concept of a magisterium appeals to me. The stumbling block is the familiar one for those who remain Anglicans. First, the doctrines connected with the Virgin Mary. It is not so much the doctrines themselves, as the fact that the Roman Catholic church teaches them as part of the essentials of the faith. The problem is that they cannot in all honesty be found in scripture, at least not in the form taught by the magisterium of the Church. Secondly, the position of the Pope. I can well accept the Pope as primus inter pares, especially of the Western Church, but not that he is an oracle in his own right. As to the Orthodox Church, again I find aspects of this hugely attractive: its spirituality, the power at once spiritual and aesthetic of its worship – Russian basses singing in church can be spine tingling. I love icons and find them a very helpful focus for devotion. I was fortunate to work on a book of readings through the Christian year with Bishop Kallistos of Diocleia,[68] to meet Metropolitan Anthony of Sourozh, and to have Father Alex Fostiropoulos and his wife, Patricia, as lovely friends. The Orthodox church shares some of the Anglican criticisms of the papacy. But I am not a Slav or a Greek and my awareness of the manifest faults and failings of the Church of England have never been strong enough to impel me towards an English Orthodox congregation. Furthermore, Orthodoxy, rooted as it is in particular national expressions, shares some of the disputatiousness of nation states. As Archbishop Zizioulas was once heard to say: "Ah, Orthodoxy, so beautiful, so beautiful. Why did God give it to the Orthodox?" So I remain an Anglican, at least knowing that the Church of England is not God's last word for his church. On the positive side I warm to the words of a revered Anglo Catholic priest to the superior of a religious community. "You know, Mother, the Church of England is the only part of the Catholic Church which is open to the future." It is this which has enabled us to take on board the ordination of women and in most places a *de facto* acceptance of gay partnerships as well as other changes.

The Church of England is part of the worldwide Anglican Communion and I have had both good and dispiriting experiences of this. The good experience was my membership of the Anglican Peace and Justice Network. This was a small group, only 15 or so, of people in Anglican churches at the forefront of their church in work for peace and justice. This kept us in touch with some of the very difficult situations in which the church is ministering, as well as some brave responses to them. It was through this that I met Luis Prado, the Bishop of Pelotas in the South of Brazil, with whom I became close friends. It was his anger that first of all impressed me. We were meeting in Singapore and the main subject of our discussions was Third World debt which was literally crippling the economy of many Third World and middle income economies. These loans, often taken out by corrupt dictators some years before, resulted in massive interest payments having to be paid for years afterwards instead of on much needed health and education needs. At the end of our meeting we had the usual discussion about when we should next meet, and those of us from developed countries suggested the usual period of three years or so. At this point Luis exploded in wrath saying that in his country this was literally a matter of life and death and we needed to meet with much more urgency. It is worth recalling that one of the great mass movements of our time, initiated by the churches and the aid agencies, the "drop the debt" campaign, did in the end achieve significant debt reductions for Third World countries.

One meeting of the Peace and Justice Network was held in Pelotas. On the journey down from Porto Allegro we were struck by how rich and fertile the land was compared with the very dry North East of Brazil. Odd to find an Anglican Diocese in the South of Brazil but in the nineteenth century it was a trading centre for British merchants. Luis took us around some of his projects. One was a collective for fishermen. Another was a collective of local farmers who were being brought together to resist the blandishment of the tobacco firms who wanted to impose a monoculture of tobacco on their farms. Apart from any scruples they might have about tobacco it would put them totally in the power of these companies. Most impressive was the settlement of about 30 families of the rural landless poor, of which there were about four million at the time. Brazil, one of the richest countries in the world, was and is in the hands of an oligarchy of wealthy ruling families.

These rural poor were squatting on some of the unused land, where they had built simple shacks to live in. Although they only had dirt floors, I was impressed by the cleanliness of everything – they made their own soap. They were sustained by mutual support, so that, for example, when one of these shacks burnt down with the loss of all possessions all the other families rallied round to rebuild and make good the losses. Particularly impressive was the leader of this community of families – a woman in her early thirties – reminding us of the key role women are playing in leadership roles in the developing world. Deeply moving was the procession of these families when they came to meet us, walking over the heathland singing simple faith songs, each with small posies of picked wild flowers to give us. Sadly, Luis, very much a hero of mine, died young.

I was also a member of the Anglican Consultative Council. This was an elected body of about 80 people from around the Communion, one of the "bonds of communion", the strands that, together with the Primates' Meeting, the Lambeth Conferences and the role of the Archbishop of Canterbury, keep the communion together. The ACC was more representative than the Primates' Meeting and less unwieldly than Lambeth and was a good body to be a member of, though it did not have any real power. One meeting was in Hong Kong where I found the Anglican church very impressive with its large number of schools and social projects all run very efficiently. Also enjoyable was our meeting in Panama with its colourful people. A surprising memory from my time there is the big party which was given in our honour. This included a band playing and dancing. Watching the dancing was a very dour faced British Ambassador next door to his wife, a stunning West African beauty, who was looking equally glum. I could not bear it, so went up to her and asked her to dance. Everyone looked on amazed at the skill and liveliness of our dancing. Not a dancing man, I have not danced like that before or since.

The Lambeth Conferences, held every ten years for all bishops in the Communion, was not such a happy experience. In 1988 not only did Jo have a major psychotic episode in the middle of the conference resulting in her having to be sectioned in a local hospital but I had a very testing piece of business to steer through. Before the conference when I had been at King's, I called together a small group to produce a document on Jewish Christian relations for approval by Lambeth. This called for a radically new relationship built on the great truths of faith and hope that we hold in common. When we got to Lambeth, it immediately ran into trouble. First, the Bishops from the Middle

East were very unhappy about the concentration on Judaism and its links with the state of Israel. Secondly, evangelical bishops thought it went too far in affirming common ground. A compromise was sought and a small group of bishops who were familiar with Islam produced another strand within the report dealing with Christian Muslim relations. Then, fortunately, David Penman, the Archbishop of Melbourne, an Arabist and someone who had the support of evangelicals worked with me as an honest broker to eventually get the document accepted. Although Lambeth documents do not usually carry much weight, this one really mattered because *The Jewish Chronicle* had built up an expectancy that it would do for the Anglian Church what *Nostra Aetate* had done for Roman Catholic Jewish relations. To have had our document rejected by Lambeth would have done a great deal of damage. So I worked hard behind the scenes with David Penman and thank goodness it was in the end accepted and still stands scrutiny, I think.[69]

On a lighter note, I missed one session and went out to ask someone what went on in it. I can still picture Michael Hare-Duke, the Bishop of St Andrews patting his pot belly and saying, "Ah, Richard, the good Lord gave me the gift of sleep." When he was a Vicar, Michael received a phone call from a desperate woman with four children who said she wanted to see him. He was all sympathy and agreed. A little later the doorbell rang. He opened it and found his wife and children. A salutary warning for all married clergy.

The 1998 Lambeth Conference was even more unhappy. It began with one of the African Bishops trying to perform an exorcism on the gay rights campaigner Richard Kirker, and went on from there. I was in the subsection dealing with the gay issue and worked with Bob Hardy, the Bishop of Lincoln, to try to soften the hard line that was emerging in the document and resolutions. When it came to the vote on the notorious resolution 2, 10, I voted in favour of it on the grounds that we had made it less bad than it had been, especially the supporting paper, and it was good to try to be united as a conference. This was an error of judgement which I regret. I should have rejected it as did a small number of other bishops.

Despite its obvious failings I find myself still in the Church of England and glad to be part of the Anglican Communion. And this I see as part of the wider fellowship of the one, holy, Catholic and Apostolic church. But the church means much more than this to me. It matters deeply to me that I stand with the whole company of Christian people in the past, the long tradition of those faithful in their own times and who now rejoice with us but in a greater light on another shore. It also means much that I stand with Christian people round the word today and with all people in their anguish and joy. A priest one told an enquirer, "You will find it difficult to find God through the church. But you may find the church through God." That reflects my experience, I have found the church through God.

When I was at Cuddesdon, Bob Runcie warned us against what he called picking nosegays out of the psalms, favourite, inspiring texts. Rather, we should see the psalter whole. For, as I have increasingly come to believe over the years the psalter is the voice of Christ in humanity crying out to the Father. The psalms express every possible mood: anger, despair, joy, bitterness, trust, hope and joy. This is first of all Christ in his people, his body of Christ on earth, but the presence of Christ is not confined to those who believe in him. He united the whole of humanity to himself. So in the psalms if it is first of all the voice of Christ in his people, it is also his voice in all whom he is calling to himself, the whole of humanity. There is no way the psalter can be said in a way that is always meaningful to an individual at every particular point in their lives, though of course it does fit remarkably well on some occasions when it does reflect our mood at the time. But if it is said in solidarity with humanity as a whole, caught up in violence, oppression and despair, as we are; and also in joy and thanksgiving, it is indeed a voice for all times and circumstances. And it is this because it is first of all the voice of the Christ who has united himself with us.

A key text for me is 1, John, 1, 3. Referring to the Divine Life revealed in Jesus the writer says: "We declare to you what we have seen and heard so that you also may have fellowship with us; and truly our fellowship is with the Father and with his Son Jesus Christ."

The word translated fellowship here, and sometimes as Communion, is in Greek *koinonia*. It is used twice in the text, and the crucial point is that to come into the communion of the church is to be taken also in the communion with God. It is a mystical communion in which the human and divine are brought together in a mutual indwelling.

So I find that the line in the wonderful post communion prayer in the Book of Common Prayer service of Holy Communion sums up how I feel. We thank God that "we are very members

80th birthday walk in the Chilterns, with friends. Left to right: Fiona Barnett, Christine Risebero, David Wilson, Piers Plowright, Derek Watson, Simon Jenkins, Anthony Neuberger, Natasha Wilson, me, Geoffrey Barnett, Hannah Jenkins, Mark Harries, Adam Roberts, Shirley Williams, Bill Risebero, Julia Neuberger.

incorporate in the mystical body of thy son, which is the blessed company of all faithful people". This is also the reason why I am always drawn by the wonderful icon of Andrei Rublev based on the scene of the hospitality of Abraham to the three angels. The church has always seen this both as a pointer to God as Holy Trinity, and the Divine Banquet to which we are invited. For as the viewer looks at the exquisite classically flowing figures of the angels round the table, they too are invited to sit and eat. It is a good icon to have in the place where one normally eats as a reminder that every meal is a sacrament and foretaste of that banquet; the life of God himself in which we are invited to share and who has come to dwell in us.

Chapter 24

Faith in a sceptical age

People sometimes ask believers if they have doubts. Doubts is not quite the right word. Better is, "challenging questions". Every time I read or hear of another horror: parents neglecting or even murdering their children, women being raped in war, people being tortured, I am challenged by the thought, "Can this world really be the creation of a wise and loving power?" That question never goes away. Indeed as T.S. Eliot, following Pascal, argued, the more mature the faith, the more searching that question will be. It is just because I believe the world *is* the creation of a wise and loving power that the challenge is so searing.

The starting point for any thoughtful human being must be the mystery of their own existence. Here am I, held in being above the abyss of nothingness. There could be nothing, but here I am. This is the overwhelming, astonishing fact. Of course we know we have come about as a result of the process of evolution but that does not take away from the extraordinary fact that something exists rather than nothing. And it is the same whether we are thinking of the Big Bang more than thirteen billion years ago or now. It would be the same if scientists discovered there was another physical state before the Big Bang. Something exists rather than nothing. The best poets, painters and novelists are sometimes able to convey the sense of mystery and astonishment that evokes.

If there was a wise and loving power behind the universe we could make sense of the mystery of existence. "Let there be", came the word, and universe came into being, *ex nihilo,* out of nothing, as Judaism, Christianity and Islam proclaim. We remain suspended above the abyss of nothingness because moment by moment we are held in existence by the ground of all being. I said it would make sense, in that we could understand why we are here *if* there was such a ground of being – but we can never prove that our existence makes sense. It might be totally senseless, meaningless. We can never prove that the world makes sense, nor for that matter can we prove that it doesn't. The reason quite simply is that in order to show that the universe is the product of a rational purpose we would have to have a standard of comparison. Only if we had one universe that came about by a rational purpose and one that didn't could we look at the universe we are in and decide into which of the two categories it fitted, designed or undesigned. For this reason I am as sceptical of arguments in favour of a creator God as I am of those against the notion. For example, in recent years the "anthropological principle" has sometimes been evoked to claim there is a God. This suggest that the world is so finely tuned for the origin of life that if the tiniest detail were different we would not have emerged. But, again, to make this claim plausible we would have to have a standard of comparison, which we have not got. By definition there is only one universe. Even if we believe there is a multiverse, there is only one multiverse. There are no other multiverses with which to compare this one.

So no proof is available either way. However, a believer claims that her or his faith makes sense of the mystery of our existence and the existence of every leaf on every tree and every atom in every grain of sand.

This belief also makes sense of many other important aspects of our life, the experience of beauty, for example. Of course there is an evolutionary explanation of why we have a capacity to appreciate beauty and no doubt it has to do with sex and reproduction much as it does with peacocks. But there is something about the experience of beauty, whether it is in a grand mountain range or a tranquil stream that draws and tantalises us, that takes us out of ourselves. The believer sees this having its final focus and home in the one St Augustine addressed as "O Thou beauty most ancient and withal so fresh".

So it is with our moral sense. Again it is the product of evolution but what we experience is something absolutely fundamental to our being. Unless we are a psychopath, we will be conscious of at least some moral imperatives. "There is honour even among thieves." For a believer this moral imperative finds its root in the will of a good God who calls us to grow in goodness. Then thirdly, the same principle applies to the way we seek the truth whether in a court of law or of life itself. We are truth seeking animals and to think that one opinion is as good as another is not so much to sell our human birthright for a mess of pottage as to throw it away altogether. For a believer, that search for truth is a golden thread that winds its way to God, the source of all truth as he is of all beauty and goodness. For in him they exist in sublime conjunction in what we call "Glory".

So my faith is a rational faith, in that it makes sense of things. It makes sense of why I exist in the first place and why it is that our capacity to appreciate beauty, make morally based decisions and seek the truth are so important to us. But to stress, this cannot be any kind of proof because there is no logically compelling reason I can give as to why things should make sense.

What so often does not seem to make sense, which does not fit the picture of a wise and loving rational power behind things is the existence of so much evil and suffering. It does not seem compatible with such a claim. Understandably this is the reason so many people lose a faith they once had or find it impossible to have faith in the first place. This for me has always been *the* big question. The idea that science undermines religious belief is absurd. Most great scientists in the past have been religious believers, and many distinguished ones are today. Nor does philosophy undermine it. As shown above, all philosophy can do is leave the matter open. But the existence of so much evil and suffering is a challenge that never goes away.

But before considering that issue, a word must be said about the definition of the three letters G O D and the limitations of all religious language. The orthodox belief of all theists is that God is the eternal and self-sufficient primary cause of all secondary causes. He is not an item in the world of items but the ground of all items. He is not a thing in the world of things but the source of all things. He is not a cause in the world of causes but the primary cause of all secondary causes. Our minds are so far from being able to imagine or picture this reality that again it is orthodox belief to say that in himself God is totally unknowable and incomprehensible. This means that all we can do is point to God in words which will always be limited; words which will be as false as they are true. Believers claim to be able to enter into a relationship with God. But clearly God is not a person in any ordinary sense. Jews and Christians address God as Father. But there are obviously more ways in which that image is untrue than ways in which it is true. It is an image that encourages us to pray with a sense of intimacy, trust, and receptivity. It cannot do more than that.

We have to use words, as that is all we have, but their limitations always need to be borne in mind, especially in this next section.

Evelyn Waugh's wonderful satirical novel *Decline and Fall* is about a school master who had once been a priest but who had lost his faith. He could see how everything followed logically, from the creation of the world to the use of incense but could never answer the question as to why God had created the world in the first place. I can have a guess at the answer to that question, and it has to do with God's essential nature as self-giving and self-bestowing love. But the question which troubles me, given the inevitability of suffering in a world of freely moving forces, and the inescapability of evil in a world where people are free to make choices that have a moral dimension is: was God justified in creating such a world?

This is the question which is implicit in Ivan Karamazov's famous remark quoted earlier. After telling some horrific stories of cruelty to children he turns to his brother and says, "It is not God I don't believe in, Alyosha, I just return him the ticket." Ivan then sketches out the picture of a wonderful heaven and argues that even that could not justify the amount of suffering on the way to it. In other words it would have been better for God not to have created the world in the first place. He should not have brought the world into existence if that was the price that had to be paid for it.

That is the challenge that has haunted me ever since I first read Dostoevsky some 60 years ago. I believe it can only be faced, and faith retained, on the basis of a full Christian orthodoxy. That of course poses a question about what this is and how one would distinguish between the essential and inessentials of faith. My criterion is a simple one. An essential of the faith is a belief which, if it was rejected, would see the whole edifice of Christian faith come tumbling down. This allows for a good number of traditional beliefs to be treated in symbolic terms, if so desired. For example, the belief that Jesus was born of a virgin mother. It is possible for someone truly to believe in the Incarnation of God in Jesus without necessarily believing in the Virgin birth, but to deny that Jesus is truly and fully God and truly and fully human in one unified person is to deny an essential. This is because it is only God himself who can unite our lives to his divinity and only if he is fully human that he can do this. If someone believes this but says they think Jesus came about by the ordinary process of human reproduction and the story of the Annunciation is a beautiful way of depicting God's initiative in bringing about our redemption, it seems to me they are holding fast to an essential. I should stress I am not trying to draw boundaries as to who should be regarded as a Christian or who not, simply trying to make my own position clear. Again, to be clear I am happy to leave the story of the

Virgin Birth where it is without raising the dust of what would be a distracting debate.

The second essential, as I indicated in an earlier chapter, is the Resurrection of Jesus Christ. I do not believe the Ascension is in the same category and again this can be seen as a symbolic way of trying to say that the Jesus who was here in flesh and blood is now present as God is present: present at every point in time, in every place, to every person. He has been raised to a universal contemporaneity.

But though we use symbolic language about the Resurrection of Christ, for again it is the only language we have got, we are here talking about a real event which was both in time and which transcends time, comparable not to the raising of Lazarus but only to the creation of the universe *ex nihilo* in the first place and the transfiguration of all things at the end into the stuff of glory. We are talking here in the language of symbolic realism. The language here is symbolic but it is about a reality. Christ was truly raised from the dead in what St Paul called "a spiritual body" and appeared to his followers in ways they could recognise and in terms of a call to further discipleship. If people want to call this an "objective vision" that is okay by me as long as the emphasis in on the word "objective". Or if they wish to picture a hologram made from the light of eternity, again that is okay by me.

The reason that belief in the Resurrection of Christ is an essential of the faith is because of the great claims made by Jesus himself. He proclaimed that the long-awaited rule of God in human affairs, the kingdom of God, was present in his ministry and its fulfilment would come soon. He preached this message with all the sense of authority of one commissioned by God to do so and implied in his parables that the pattern of his ministry, which was one of including in the kingdom those on the margins, was the pattern of God himself. He addressed God in intimate terms as Father and suggested that his own presence was a *Kairos* time, a time of judgement when people had to make a radical choice one way or another. But he ended up tortured on the cross. Without the resurrection, Jesus would understandably be seen as an inspired prophet and great moral teacher but one who was mistaken in his fundamental beliefs. His Resurrection is, in the phrase of the German theologian Wolfhart Pannenberg, "the retroactive validation" of his message and mission.

The third central pillar of the Christian faith is a belief in life after death. This is not because of a desire by the individual to survive death but because the whole of the Hebrew Scriptures, and especially the psalms, is about the ultimate triumph of the purpose of God and the vindication of the devout people who trust him but who so often lose out in the world as it is now. The reason why a glorious life after death is central is because it is about the vindication of God and those good people who trust him despite all the wickedness in the world. It is for this reason that I find it strange that so many people claim to believe in God but sit light to any prospect of an afterlife.

That eternal life is obviously beyond anything we can imagine now. But there are two things about it I would want to affirm. I have come to believe that all will be saved, that is, everyone will be reconciled and won over to share in the life of God. When St Paul says that God will be "all in all" it means what it says. God's loving presence and purpose will fill and irradiate all people and things.[70]

Secondly, there is nothing sentimental about this. People sometimes choose a quotation for their funeral service suggesting that death is just a slipping away into the next room. How could it be when it will mean the stripping away of the veil between us and the all holy God? We cannot ignore the sombre warnings of judgement in the Bible, though of course they have to be understood not literally but symbolically. What they symbolise is an intense awareness of the darkness of evil and our role in it, leading to searing self-knowledge. As so often T.S. Eliot in the *Four Quartets* gets it right. The theme of going into the dark runs through the poem, the darkness of death and painful remorse. But the two dominant images at the end are fire and love, the fire of self-knowledge which is at the same time the fire of Divine love. In the end the fire and the love are one as they enfold the great white rose of redeemed humanity.

Some people will find it odd that I feel so committed to Christian orthodoxy in the sense that I have outlined it. There are two reasons for this. First, I find it impossible to hold on to any faith except on the basis of those essentials. This is because of the extent of evil and suffering in the world and the fierce case this makes against the claim that there is a loving power behind it all. The case against God is so strong that it is only on the basis of the full Christian story that I hold on. This story says that we have been created in the image of God, that is, able to think and choose, love and pray and we are called to grow into God's likeness. In order to achieve this, God himself came to share our nature, overcome evil from within history and so unite our lives with his risen life that we come to share his divine nature. Finally, there is an ultimate state that is so wondrous and glorious that the suffering along the way somehow drops away in the light of the sublime beauty and supreme ecstasy of that life in which God will be all in all. It is in the light of that full panoply of faith that I am able to live with the challenge posed by evil and suffering.

The second reason I hold to that wholeness of faith is that I find it so sublime. I cannot imagine a more wonderful and exciting story. It was this sense that G.K. Chesterton was able to convey in his book *Orthodoxy*. This does not of itself make it true but it means I find orthodox Christian faith hugely interesting in a way I find very liberal interpretations of the faith not only inadequate in facing the intellectual challenge of suffering but so dull. And if someone asks me how I am able to believe these astonishing things, I can only reply that there is nothing more astonishing than the fact of life itself. The fact that there is something rather than nothing is amazing. And there is kind of congruity of awe and wonder between this and the amazing story told by Christians. The real puzzle is why so many people seem to take life for granted, as though it was ordinary, when in fact it is quite extraordinary.

The section began by defining God as the eternal and self-sufficient primary cause of all secondary causes. In the light of the Christian faith I would now add, God is good, all good, my true and everlasting good.

Christmas 2021. Left to right: grandsons Toby and Ben, son Mark, grandson Luke, daughter Clare, granddaughter Sophie, and daughter-in-law Cilla.

Chapter 25

"This world is not conclusion"[71]

"Bless what there is for being"

When W.H. Auden was going through an unhappy period in his life he began a poem called "Precious Five" wanting to curse the sky in anger and despair. It ends, however, with the refrain that we have to "Bless what there is for being". When I discussed this poem in an earlier book, I suggested that in facing the suffering and evil of the world we are forced to ask: are we still able to bless what there is for being? Or, more particularly, are we able to bless God for our own being? Am I able to bless God that I am Richard Harries, and I have lived?[72]

Of course we all have some regrets. I wish I had a better auditory memory. I wish Jo's life had not been hurt by her bipolar disorder. I wish I had been a better person. But, yes, I am indeed able to bless God for my being, indeed I regard myself as very blessed. I am conscious of how extremely fortunate I have been. Even from a human point of view, I have done a job that has brought a great deal of fulfilment, enabling me to express and develop different aspects of my person as pastor and leader, and which has enabled me to express the creative side of my nature in writing and broadcasting. As described in the first chapter, I was blessed with parents who loved me and gave me a secure and stable upbringing. I have a brother and sister whom I greatly respect and of whom I am very fond. I have a lovely wife and wonderful children. Recently, doing something for Jo, she accused me of being impatient. This was very unusual, for she is normally equable. When I protested, she said, "You should be very pleased to have me with you," which I am. Finally, we have wonderful, supportive friends.

Life now is much more constricted than it was. Jo has vascular dementia and is in a wheelchair with everything needing doing for her. It is amazing how equable and cheerful she remains despite the terrible frustrations and indignities of her life. We still entertain regularly, and friends much enjoy her company when they come to tea with her. Although her mind can wander away, so that she can think she is in her grandmother's house, or needs to go and see her mother, now long dead, her smile is still beguiling. We have good carers to get her up and put her to bed and all the medical aids that modern technology can provide, Stannah stairlifts, hoists, turners etc. and a car with a ramp that can have a wheelchair pushed into the back. Most especially our son, Mark, Cilla his wife and three grandsons live two streets away, and our daughter, Clare, and granddaughter, Sophie, when not in lockdown come over from France where they live, to be with us for school holidays. In a globalised world so many grandparents have to put up with their grandchildren living in America or Australia or somewhere else far away, therefore it is a wonderful blessing to have ours closer, even though they are all so busy we sometimes have to book them up in advance. Another great blessing is the proximity of a local church where we feel at home, St Mary's, Barnes. It is close enough for me to push Jo for a Eucharist on Sundays. Every morning at 8.45 we have a service of morning prayer with a small group of regulars. And on Sundays I have the privilege of celebrating the Eucharist or preaching on a regular basis.

I have been greatly very blessed with my wife, Jo, our son, Mark, who is a consultant oncologist at Guy's and St Thomas's hospitals and daughter, Clare, who gave up her successful career as an academic psychologist to live a different life in France. I am hugely proud of our grandsons, Luke, Toby and Ben, all making their way in the world and granddaughter, Sophie, who is already making waves.

Not least of course there is the divine grace which supports and permeates all our lives, and the gift of faith to try to live by it. This is not just one thing in a list of other things but rather that which is in and through them all, enabling them to be blessings. Dr Johnson once wrote that, "The only end of writing is to enable readers better to enjoy life or better to endure it." We could say that faith has the same effect. It enhances the ordinary pleasures of life enabling them truly to be, and to remain, pleasures. It helps us get through the disappointments and difficulties we all encounter with courage and hope. Christ, we might say is both our keel and anchor. The keel enabling us to stay upright when sailing well in a good wind, the anchor enabling us to stay firm and not get swept away in a storm. It's odd, though, that a sailing image should come to mind as I am an incompetent sailor, combining, as my wife says, total confidence with total ignorance, a fatal combination.

A fraught future

Not only has my personal life been blessed in so many ways but the times through which I have lived has spared my generation in this country so much of the anguish that continues to grip the rest of the world. We grew up in the shadow of World War II and have always been haunted by the terrible fatalities of World War I, but despite the civil strife and violence of Northern Ireland and intermittent terrorism we have not experienced the major conflicts, civil wars and disasters that ravage so much of the globe. I have always described myself as a hopeful realist. However, as I look to the future of the world I aim to be realistic about its risks. It continues to be a very dangerous world, with a serious chance of nuclear weapons being used at some point. In particular I see a serious clash with China coming at some point in the future over Taiwan. No less risky is the increasing use of cyber attacks, with the possibility of whole states being brought to a standstill. As a result of climate change there is potential conflict over the world's resources, especially food and water. Trying to manage these dangers human beings remain much as they always have been, largely driven by the desire for money, power, fame and sex. At the time of writing there is also the pandemic of COVID-19, with the country coming out of a long lockdown, the financial consequences of Brexit and the disastrous series of failures over Afghanistan. We do not know how all this will affect us in the long term. However, this is not all that motivates us. There is a capacity in all of us to transcend narrow self-interest and take others into account, sometimes indeed the capacity to sacrifice that self-interest for them. The problem, as classically exposed in Reinhold Niebuhr's *Moral Man and Immoral Society,* is that whilst we may have that capacity as individuals, it is not a feature of organised groups, whether a business or a nation. Here it is power that counts, economic or military. And here there is a particularly depressing feature of our times. For World War II was followed by the active desire to establish international organisations and institutions that would by discussion and agreement tame some of the worst features of national power seeking in the interest of the common good. The European Union was one such achievement, and now we have left it. Furthermore, liberal democracy is now under threat by autocratic governments in a number of countries. So my dear grandchildren inherit a very uneasy and unstable world, fraught with dangers of many kinds. But I remain hopeful about the world. I do not believe in inevitable or automatic progress and there is nothing so bad that it cannot get worse. At the same time, there is nothing that cannot be redeemed, for God is ceaselessly at work through people of good will seeking to draw some good out of the mess we make of things. If there is the seed of evil in every advance, there is the soul of good that remains in every setback.

If the first fortunate feature of my lifetime has been the absence of major conflict on our soil, the second has been in its medical advances. We are now able to be kept healthier for longer than ever before and I have certainly benefited from that like most of our generation. As a family we have been and continue to be wonderfully well served by the NHS. Here too there are issues for the future, not least the increasing number of old people who will need care, care which needs paying for. More widely than that the most extraordinary advances, if they are advances, are now floated as possibilities for the future. We can envisage designer babies, the replacement of all our body parts, the renewal of our cells, the reproduction of the algorithms of the brain all combining to create beings that could live a very long time, if not endlessly. Nothing can be ruled out. But we will need to think hard about the ethical dilemmas raised by these developments and the desirability, or not, of some of these steps. But whatever those developments might be, they do not amount to the Kingdom of God, nor can they compare with that new life in Christ which we can enter now and which death cannot take away.

Can the Church of England Survive?

I also bring this hopeful realism to bear when I reflect on the future of the Christian Church. Secular pundits still tend to predict the inevitable decline and eventual demise of religion. But if we take the world as a whole the story looks very different, with religion growing rapidly in many places. Confining myself to Christianity and the Church of England in particular the following factors, so often ignored, need noting.

The dynamic centre of Christian faith was for many centuries in the East. Until the fall of Constantinople in 1453, the Byzantine world had for 1500 years or so been a glittering Christian civilisation that far outshone anything going on in Europe. Then, in the eleventh and twelfth centuries the alliance of Christianity and power came together in the Normans and the dynamic energy of faith moved first to Europe and then the

United States. Now it may very well be moving to China where, it is predicted, there will within 50 years be more Christians than in the whole of Europe and America put together. Perhaps the next Christian civilisation will be located there, in China. Worldwide, both Christianity and Islam are growing. But clearly in England there has been a decline in attendance in the Church of England in recent decades. But again this has to be seen in a longer historical perspective and against the background of the recent decline in all traditional institutions. Not long ago it was noted that churches were closing at a slower rate than local newspapers. The decline in membership of political parties, for example, has been far more dramatic than that of the Church of England. Against this general decline in establishment institutions, it has held up quite well.

Then again, there was no golden period of belief from which everything has fallen away, at least not since the seventeenth-century civil war, the last time that the English as a whole were passionate about religion. Jonathan Swift, the Dean of St Patrick's, Dublin, for example, in his wonderful satirical piece "An argument against abolishing Christianity" written in 1708 said that, "I freely own, that all appearances are against me. The system of the Gospel, after the fate of other systems is generally antiquated and exploded; and the mass of body of the common people, among whom it seems to have had its latest credit, are now grown as much ashamed of it, as their betters."[73] His main arguments for its retention was to comfort children at night and to give the wits of the age something to laugh and sneer at. There was indeed a new seriousness about religion in the nineteenth century but the Victorians built too many large churches which have never been full. The result is that there was from the start a built-in sense in the Church of England of a falling away from some period of universal observance, which has never been the case. A combination of *fin de siècle* mentality, followed by World War I drained much of this religion away. Adrian Hastings in his history of Christianity in England in the twentieth century notes that amongst the ruling political leaders around in the early part of the century there was not a single orthodox Christian amongst them.[75] When in 1927 T.S. Eliot converted to an Anglo-Catholic form of faith, he was anxious to meet the American scholar Paul Elmer More, who had come to faith by the same route as himself because "I might almost say that I never met any Christians until after I had made up my mind to become one."[76] We now live in an even more seriously secular society, with constant denigration or belittling of religion in the media. If a writer begins as they sometimes do, "I was brought up as a Catholic" they usually quickly qualify this by saying that of course they don't believe it now. Indeed one gay novelist, Michael Arditti, who is also a Christian said that it was now easier in our society to come out as gay than as a Christian. When Rowan Williams became Archbishop of Canterbury, he said his great ambition was to recapture the imagination of our society for the Christian faith. That task we have so far failed to do. In addition there is now a widespread ignorance about the faith. When I was a curate in Hampstead, the number of churchgoers was not significantly higher, but you could count on a basic knowledge of the main Christian images and stories in society as a whole. That has now gone.

Before the Emperor Constantine was converted in the early fourth century, creating that uneasy alliance of Christian faith and political power which has shaped our civilisation, a powerless Christian faith had already captured a large portion of the hearts and minds of the Roman world by peaceful preaching and teaching alone. I remain excited by the sublime beauty and truth of the message. And the task of the church is to teach it whether the times are propitious or unpropitious.

More problematic is the church which has to carry this message. During my time in ministry the number of church goers has steadily declined and from a human point of view the future looks bleak. In 2012 I conducted a review of the Church in Wales, ably assisted by Professor Charles Handy, the business guru, and Professor Patricia Peattie from the Episcopal Church of Scotland. Over a year we listened to large gatherings all over Wales. Liz Handy, Charles's wife, who controlled his dairy complained to him that it was worse than having a mistress. Our main conclusion was that the parish as we have known it for the last 1000 years is no longer viable. Instead there should be area ministries of 20 to 30 parishes served by three or four stipendiary clergy. There would still be a congregation in each parish but led by a self-supporting minister or lay person. The Church in Wales accepted this and is moving slowly to implement it. At the time of writing, the Church of England is having to look at similarly radical proposals. The main driver is finance. With diminishing congregations who is going to pay for the clergy, on top of the huge amounts people have to raise every year for the historic buildings?

A final surprise

Now I am winding down I am conscious of how very lucky I have been – blessed I would say – in having had a very strong sense of direction for my life.[77] As described earlier, I was originally lined up for a career in the army but then, much to my surprise and the shock of my parents, I had an overwhelming sense that God was calling me to be ordained. When I first pictured this it was in terms of parish ministry. A ministry in which broadcasting, writing and engaging in some of the major issues of our time was in no way planned but has constantly come as a series of surprises. But now I am "retired". At 85 I may like to think that this is the new 60 but the fact is I cannot do many of the things I once did. I have even had to give up tennis, and I walk much more slowly. What are we to make of this last period of our life? Can we talk about a special purpose here, a new vocation or calling to make something special of this time? Or is it just a matter of waiting in the departure lounge for death to take us?

Some Hindus have a rather appealing approach to the different periods of our life. The first period is the one for developing into the person we are. The second is for building a family and making a success of work. Then, when that is over, it is time to walk into the forest, strip off all the inessentials and prepare for the final phase of letting go into death. I suppose the nearest we come to that in our society is when people who are lucky enough to have a house sell up, declutter themselves of so many possessions and move into something smaller or sheltered. All very sensible but it hardly takes us into the spiritual heart of the matter.

In the Hebrew scriptures old age is regarded as a blessing. That may be but what is it for? What is my vocation now? A trilogy of novels by the American writer Kent Haruf, *Plainsong, Eventide* and *Benediction*, is about very ordinary people towards the end of their lives all described in the most minute detail. One man, Dad Lewis, who only has a short time left gets his family to drive him round the small town where he has lived all his life. They park the car by the hardware store which he owns and ran, and he counts up the number of times he went through the front door. "Fifty-five years times six days a week times 52 weeks – a lifetime," he reflects. He watches a man being served at the counter, and then finds himself in tears. Later his wife asks him why. "It was my life I was watching there," he replied, "that little bit of commerce between me and another fellow on a summer morning at the front counter. Exchanging a few words. Just that. And it wasn't nothing at all." "No, that's not right," responds his wife. "It wasn't either nothing. It was everything." His story does not end there. He calls in the two people who worked for him in the store and thanked them for all they had done, and gave them a substantial bonus, and they tell him how much he means to them. He calls in his daughter and says sorry that he did not give her all the attention he should have done when she was young. She agrees, but still says she loves him. What emerges so strongly from this exchange is what one character describes as "the precious ordinary". Dad Lewis was an ordinary person in an ordinary job with ordinary relationships, but his life did not amount to nothing. In the final phase of his life, he comes to see this and he puts the seal on it by words of thanks and regret and love. The novel is called *Benediction*. His life, however ordinary, was a blessing and it was in and through the small details of his everyday life that he was a blessing to others and others to him.

When we are old, life for all of us becomes much more a matter of ordinary routines and small details: getting up, getting dressed, having a cup of tea. For me this included until recently an early walk down the road to get a new loaf of bread from the bakery and my paper, feeling the fresh air on my cheek, seeing the sky, hearing the blackbirds. It is a time for savouring the ordinary, the precious ordinary, the small detail, for here, quite simply is the gift of life to be relished in itself for itself. It brings to mind George Herbert's description of prayer as "heaven in ordinary". Through prayer the ordinary is not only precious but it is how heaven comes to us. Linked to this is the gift of time which old age can bring and this means time for remembering and thinking. I have started to look through old photos with Jo, remembering some lovely holidays we had, some good friends, the children when they were young. "Let your last thinks all be thanks" wrote W.H. Auden in his poem "Lullaby". And as the psychologist Dr Oliver Sacks said of his friend Auden: "Wystan's mind and heart came closer and closer in the course of his life, until thinking and thanking became one and the same."

Remembering and thinking can, however, also bring dark thoughts. Dad Lewis in the novel I have just quoted remembers the time he sacked a man for dishonesty. The man then shot himself. In later years Lewis did his best to support the widow but he is still troubled by the thought that he could have handled the issue differently. When Jesus was on his own in the desert for 40 days he too had to go through an intense inner struggle. As the Son of God he had to face a fierce inner test about the nature of his vocation. So also did those Christians in the fourth century who went to live a life of prayer in the desert. Spending time on their own meant that they often had to struggle with angry inner demons. Old age, which offers time for thinking and remembering, can bring painful memories as well as good ones. Things come up from the depths. But that too is good, for it is God who is the troubler of those depths.

A feature of life for most of us who are getting old, are aches, pains and illness of one kind and another. It tends to become an inevitable part of any conversation. I heard of two musician friends who when they met up, always began, as they said, with an organ recital. On the one hand one does not want to turn into a moaner, or indeed spend one's time listening to the moans of others – on the other hand what are old friends for if you can't actually say how you are feeling to them? But still we can ask whether there might be another approach. When towards the end of his life I asked Robert Runcie the former Archbishop of Canterbury, then suffering from cancer, how he was, he replied "dying but cheerful". This is an approach powerfully put by W.B. Yeats in his poem "Sailing to Byzantium".

> An aged man is but a paltry thing,
> A tattered coat upon a stick, unless
> Soul clap its hands and sing, and louder sing
> For every tatter in its mortal dress,

I love this poem but it sets a hard challenge. It suggests that as an old man I am just a tattered coat upon a stick, a scarecrow, unless my soul can sing. That seems just possible but it goes on to say that I have to louder sing for all those aches, pains and illnesses, all those tatters in my mortal dress. That seems a bit much when health is rightly so important to us and most of us are much easier to live with when we are feeling well. But as a Christian I am called to enter more deeply into the mystery of Christ's passion and resurrection. There I can hope to catch the strains of another kind of music, a new song of all things overcome, of divine love on its way to final victory. Perhaps I can sing in harmony with this and be taken into that unbroken communion with God which Christ pioneered and made possible for us.

Meanwhile there are all the little routines of the day, the ordinary tasks to be performed. It is here especially I think we can learn to live with a new richness and depth, an awareness and intensity that makes this period of our life a special blessing. Someone I knew who was bedridden with crippling arthritis for many years of her life was at the same time one of the most alive, alert people I have known. One of the things which helped her was simply looking out of her window at the birdfeeder and watching the birds. She didn't just notice, she looked. Especially moving on this was the playwright Dennis Potter when he was suffering from cancer. In his last interview with Melvyn Bragg he said that when he looked out of the window he didn't just notice the white blossom.

I *see* it is the whitest, frothiest, blossosmest blossom there ever could be. Things are both more trivial than they ever were and more important than they ever were, and the difference between the trivial and the important does not seem to matter. But the nowness of everything is absolutely wondrous. There is no way of telling you but the glory of it, if you like the comfort of it, the reassurance ... the fact is, if you see the present tense, boy do you see it! And boy can you celebrate it.

227

The special gift of old age is to slow us down, give us time, and our vocation is to see the detail, to savour the ordinary, to celebrate the gift of life itself for itself in all its minute particulars. In this way we can come to be, like the colours of autumn, a specially rich blessing to others. That is my ideal, anyway.

The modern view of what it is to be a human being reinforces the biblical understanding that we are psychosomatic unities; body, mind and spirit all bound up together. So when we die we really die, dust goes to dust. I have no particular interest in some spiritual part of me surviving this dissolution, even if it were possible. But I do have a passionate commitment to the good purpose of God and trust that his love cannot finally fail. All through the Bible there is the hope that one day his kingdom will come, all that is wrong will be righted and everything will flourish as God intends. I also believe that the person I truly am is known to God and is as it were lodged in his heart. In Christ he has promised that this person will be clothed in immortality. So I am not fearful of death, though like most human beings I am apprehensive about the process of dying. I hope to die with the words of Jesus in my mind, if not on my lips, "Father, into thy hands I commit my spirit", the prayer from Psalm, 31, which every Jewish mother taught their children to say at night. This is to face death in hope. I have no idea how this hope might be fulfilled, nor do I need to know.[78]

No one would accuse the poet R.S. Thomas of being sentimental. On the contrary, his poetic vision is bleak. But in one poem he envisages coming across a village in the Welsh hills and after a long journey he catches one truth by surprise "that there is everything to look forward to".[79] To let go into death in an act of trust and a spirit of hope – with everything to look forward to. Emily Dickinson put it wonderfully when she wrote.

I believe we shall be in some manner cherished by our Maker – that the one who gave us this remarkable earth has the power still further to surprise that which he caused. Beyond that all is silence.[80]

Mine has been a life taken by surprise. The surprise of a dramatic and irresistible call to be ordained; the constant surprise of new blessings and new areas to explore and write about. I believe with Emily Dickinson that God has the power still further to surprise us.[81]

Endnotes

1. The first line of a wonderful poem by Emily Dickinson, *The Complete Poems,* ed. Thomas H. Johnson, Faber 1975, p. 501.
2. David N Thomas, *Dylan Thomas, Poetry Wales Press,* 2000. Anyone who would like to read my reminiscences should drop me a note at: harriesr@parliament.uk.
3. Richard Harries, *Haunted by Christ: modern writers and the struggle for faith,* SPCK, 2018
4. He was adamant that we should take tragedy seriously. See my "Christianity and Tragedy" in *Companion to Theology and the Arts,* ed. Imogen Atkins and Stephen Garrett, Edinburgh, T&T Clark, 2022.
5. I produced an anthology of his writings. *The One Genius: readings through the year with Austin Farrer,* selected by Richard Harries, London, SPCK 1987. See also my commemoration sermon in *The Human Person in God's world: studies to commemorate the Austin Farrer Centenary,* ed. Brian Hebblethwaite and Douglas Hedley, London, SCM, 1988. Together with Stephen Patten I have tried to introduce Farrer to a new generation of scholars in *Austin Farrer, a Prophetic Legacy,* ed Richard Harries and Stephen Platten, London, SCM, 2020.
6. W. H. Vanstone, *Love's Endeavour, Love's expense,* London, Darton, Longman and Todd, 1977.
7. A talk I did on the life of Joseph McCulloch at St Mary-le-Bow is available on https://www.youtube.com/watch?v=MUdGnx5prPM.
8. The resulting publication was called *Teaching Christian Ethics,* The Advisory council for the Church's Ministry, London, SCM, 1974.
9. Later when I was at King's, I mounted a conference on Niebuhr which resulted in *Reinhold Niebuhr and the issues of*

our time, ed and intro. Richard Harries, London, Mowbray 1986. Later still, when Niebuhr was in danger of being overlooked, I worked with Stephen Platten to produce *Reinhold Niebuhr and Contemporary Politics: God and Power,* ed. Richard Harries and Stephen Platten, Oxford, OUP 2010. I sought to introduce Niebuhr in short form in *Reinhold Niebuhr reconsidered,* Grove Books 2011. It has recently been translated into Korean.

10. *What hope in an armed world?* Pickering 1982.
11. Richard Harries, *Christianity and war in a nuclear age,* London, Mowbray, 1986. See also Richard Harries "The application of Just War criteria in the period 1959–89" in *The Ethics of War* ed. Richard Sorabji and David Rodin, Farnham. Ashgate, 2006 which contains extensive footnotes with references to my own and other writing on this issue.
12. Richard Harries, "Should Trident be replaced?", in *Britain's next bomb?* ed Brian Wicker and Hugh Beach, SCM, 2006.
13. Richard Harries, *Should a Christian support guerrillas?* Guildford, Lutterworth, 1982.
14. The Lectures were published as *Prayer and the Pursuit of Happiness,* Fount, 1985, the Archbishop of Canterbury's Lent book for that year.
15. They founded the Helwel Trust which still continues to support health and well-being projects in Zululand.
16. The Bishop Simeon Trust exists in his memory to support vital work amongst vulnerable people in South Africa.
17. Richard Harries, "Power, Coercion and Morality" reprinted in Richard Harries, *Questions of Belief,* SPCK, 1995,p.116ff.
18. I drew out the implications of this in "The Christian Concept of Peace", reprinted in Richard Harries, Questions of Belief, SPCK, 1995, p. 91ff.
19. Sometimes the lectures could come together with different areas of my life in a creative way. On one cruise I had to lecture on the Gallipoli campaign, and this was a great

help when asked to deliver the annual Gallipoli Lecture, which was later published. "The de-romanticisation of war and the struggle for faith" in *The Straits of War: Gallipoli Remembered*, intro Sir Martin Gilbert, Sutton, 2000, chap 16.

20. Brian Redhead gives a warm account of my appearances on the *Today* programme in Richard Harries, *Morning has Broken: Thoughts and Prayers from BBC 4's TODAY programme*, Marshall Pickering, 1985, p. 9.

21. Richard Harries, *Prayers of Hope*, BBC, 1975, Richard Harries, *Prayers of Grief and Glory*, Lutterworth, 1979; *Morning has Broken*, Marshall Pickering, 1985, *In the Gladness of Today*, Fount 1999. See also "The Breakfast pulpit" in Paul Donovan, *All our todays: forty years of the Today Programme*, Jonathan Cape, 1997, chap 7.

22. Richard Harries, *Turning to Prayer*, Mowbray, 1978. Richard Harries, *Being a Christian*, Mowbray, 1981.Richard Harries, *Praying round the clock*, Mowbray 1983. Later I used some of the prayers from this and together with others to produce Richard Harries, *Praying the Eucharist*, SPCK, 2004.

23. Richard Harries, "My experience of women priests in the Church of England" in *Priests in mature Communities*, ed Ramón Alario, Pierre Collet, Joe Mulrooney, European Federation of Catholic Married Priests, 2015, p. 289.

24. *Religion and the News,* ed. Jolyon Mitchell and Owen Gower, Ashgate, 2012.

25. I have consistently used Just War criteria in trying to assess the legitimacy or otherwise of recent wars. See Richard Harries, "The continuing crucial relevance of Just War criteria" in *British Foreign Policy and the Anglican Church: Christian engagement with the contemporary world*, ed Timothy Blewett, Adrian Hyde-Price and Why Rees, Ashgate, 2008.

26. The best recent approach to this subject I know is by Loretta Minghella, the former Director of Christian Aid and a former First Church Estates Commissioner and now

Master of Clare College, Cambridge in *Money, Bias and the Geography of the Heart* available from the Dean's office at King's College, London. dean@kcl.ac.uk.

27. Richard Harries, *Is there a Gospel for the Rich?* Mowbray 1992.

28. Peter Brown, *Through the eye of a needle: wealth, the fall of Rome, and the making of Christianity in the West, 350–550 AD,* Princeton, 2012. Peter Brown has illuminated and transformed our understanding of late antiquity in a series of magisterial books.

29. Rowan Williams, "Things to say to psychotic dictators" in *Speaking of Faith,* ed. John Miller, Canterbury, 2016, p. 216.

30. For a full account of all this see Stephen Bates, *A Church at War: Anglicans and Homosexuality,* Hodder and Stoughton, 2005, Chapter 10.

31. Hansard, House or Lords, 15 October 1998, column1164/5.

32. On a rough calculation it is well over 5000 words. "Theology" asks that essays submitted be no longer than 3,500 words.

33. Fisher Papers, Vol. 171. p. 309ff.

34. Paul Ramsey, *Who speaks for the church?,* St Andrews Press, 1969.

35. *ibid* p. 247.

36. Ramsey papers, Vol 105, p. 271. Lord Saltoun was going to make a speech in the House of Lords critical of Ramsey, and wrote to him to make sure he quoted him accurately.

37. Ramsey Papers, Vol. 85, p. 311.

38. Richard Harries, *After the Evil, Christianity and Judaism in the Shadow of the Holocaust,* OUP, 2003, p. 129–30.

39. Richard Harries, "The Pastoral Pragmatist: Runcie as a communicator" in *Runcie: on reflection* ed. Stephen Platten, Canterbury, 2002, chap. 7.

40. *Peacemaking in a Nuclear Age,* Church of England Board for Social Responsibility, 1994.

41. Richard Harries, "Justin Welby's Leadership", *Journal of Anglican Studies,* Volume 14, issue 2, November 2016.

42. The substance of this chapter first appeared in *Theology,* Jan/Feb 2018, Vol 121. No. 1.

43. Richard Harries, *Being a Christian,* Mowbray, 1981.

44. Richard Harries, *Christ Is Risen,* Mowbray, 1987.

45. Richard Harries, *The Real God: a response to Anthony Freeman's God in Us.* Mowbray, 1994.

46. Richard Harries, "Evolution and Christian Faith in the Nineteenth Century", in *Intelligent Faith: A celebration of 150 years of Darwinian evolution,* ed. John Quenby and John MacDonald Smith, O books, 2009, p. 311ff. Richard Harries, "Half ape, half angel", in *What Makes Us Human,* ed. Charles Pasternak, One World, 2007, p. 71ff.

47. Richard Harries, "God outside the Box: on taking serious atheism seriously", in *Religion, Society and God: public theology in action,* ed. Richard Noake and Nicolas Buxton, SCM, 2013, p. 1ff.

48. Alec Vidler, *The Church in an age of Revolution,* Penguin, 1961, p. 113.

49. Richard Harries, *God outside the Box: Why spiritual people object to Christianity,* SPCK, 2002.

50. D.H. Lawrence, *Complete Poems*, ed. Vivian de Sola Pinto and Warren Roberts, 1994, Vol II, p. 622.

51. Austin Farrer, "In his image: in commemoration of C.S. Lewis", in *The Brink of Mystery,* SPCK, 1976. p. 46.

52. I wrote a little book on C.S. Lewis, *The Man and His God,* Fount, 1987. In this I acknowledge my great debt to Lewis but at the same time I offered some criticisms. I received one letter from America, where he is cult figure amongst evangelicals, more or less along the lines of how did I a mere mortal dare to criticise one of the immortals. Although my book was published in America as well Britain it was quickly dropped there!

53. Austin Farrer, *A Celebration of Faith*, Hodder and Stoughton, 1970, p. 60.

54. Hans Urs von Balthazar, *The Glory of the Lord*, vol I, T and T Clark, 1982, p. 18.

55. Richard Harries, *Art and the Beauty of God*, Mowbray, 1993.

56. Richard Harries, *A Gallery of Reflections, the Nativity of Christ: Devotional reflections on the Christmas story in art*, Lion, 1995.

57. Richard Harries, *The Passion in Art*, Ashgate, 2004.

58. Richard Harries, *The Image of Christ in Modern Art*, Ashgate, 2013.

59. Richard Harries, *The Christian Faith in 30 Images*, SPCK, 2020.

60. Richard Harries, *The Re-enchantment of Morality: wisdom for a troubled world.* SPCK, 2008.

61. Richard Harries, *Faith in Politics? Rediscovering the Christian roots of our political values*, DLT, 2010, reissued with a new introduction in 2014.

62. Richard Harries, *Haunted by Christ: modern writers and the struggle for faith*, SPCK, 2018. Later came *Hearing God in Poetry: 50 poems for Lent and Easter*, SPCK, 2021.

63. Richard Harries, *The Beauty and the Horror: searching for God in a suffering world*, SPCK, 2016.

64. See also "Christianity and Tragedy" in *A Companion to Christianity and the Arts*, ed Imogen Adkins and Stephen Garrett, T&T Clark, 2022.

65. *Dialogue with a Difference, The Manor House Group Experience*, ed. Tony Bayfield and Marcus Braybooke, SCM, 1992.

66. Richard Harries, *After the Evil: Christianity and Judaism in the Shadow of the Holocaust*, OUP, 2003.

67. *Abraham's Children: Jews, Christians and Muslims in Conversation*, Norman Solomon, Richard Harries, Tim Winter, T and T Clark, 2005.

68. *Seasons of the Spirit: readings through the Christian year,* selected and edited by George Every, Richard Harries and Kallistos Ware, SPCK, 1984.

69. "Jews, Christians and Muslims: the way of dialogue", in *The Truth shall set your free: the Lambeth Conference 1988,* p. 299ff. Church House Publishing 1988.

70. Richard Harries, "Universal Salvation", *Theology,* Vol 123 No.1 January/February 2020.

71. Emily Dickinson, *The Complete Poems,* ed. Thomas H.Johnson, Faber 1975, p. 501.

72. *The Beauty and the Horror,* p. 153.

73. Jonathan Swift, "An argument against abolishing Christianity", *Jonathan Swift,* ed. Angus Ross and David Woolley, OUP, 1984, p. 217/18.

74. Robin Gill, *The Myth of the Empty Church,* SPCK 1993.

75. Adrian Hastings, *A History of English Christianity 1920–2000.* SCM, 2001, p. 54.

76. *The Letter of T.S. Eliot, volume 4:1928–1929,* ed. Valerie Eliot and John Haffenden, Faber 2013, p. 769.

77. Much of this section was first broadcast in a talk on Old Age on Radio 4 on 12 April 2017.

78. I write more fully about Christian hope in *The Beauty and the Horror,* p. 143ff. See also "Attitudes to death in the 20th Century" reprinted in Richard Harries, *Questioning Belief,* SPCK 1995, p. 32.

79. R.S. Thomas, "Arrival" *Collected poems,* 1945–90, J.M. Dent, 1993, p. 427.

80. Thomas H. Johnson, *The Letters of Emily Dickinson,* Belknap Press of Harvard University, 1958 Letter, 785.

81. The *Shaping of a Soul* is not a straightforward biography. An account of my life and ministry within the context of our times has already been written by John Peart-Binns, and I would like to pay tribute to him for that (John S. Peart-Binns, *A Heart in my Head,* Continuum, 2007). He

wrote to me out of the blue one day asking to write my biography and we agreed to meet in York railway station where we found that over a couple of gins we got on famously. Coming from a modest background he told me that at the age of 16 he had developed a strong vocation to be an ecclesiastical biographer! To know what you want to do at that age is unusual enough but to know with such precision and on such an esoteric subject must be unique. I would also like to pay tribute to Michael Brierley my last chaplain as Bishop of Oxford. At a farewell dinner in our house to my senior staff he suddenly presented me with a *feschrift* which he had been working on for months totally unknown to me. He did a wonderful job of work in putting together a book of essays on my major interests by a range of people including Shirly Williams and Douglas Hurd (*Public Life and the Place of the Church: reflections to honour the Bishop of Oxford* ed. Michael Brierley Ashgate, 2006). In addition to these books there is a thoughtful interview by Mary Loudon (Mary Loudon, *Revelations: the clergy questioned,* Hamish Hamilton, 1994, p. 345ff).

THE NEW OPEN SPACES

Throughout the two thousand years of Christian tradition there have been, and still are, groups and individuals that exist in the margins and upon the edge of faith. But in Christianity's contrapuntal history it has often been these outcasts and pioneers that have forged contemporary orthodoxy out of former radicalism as belief evolves to engage with and encompass the ever-changing social and scientific realities. Real faith lies not in the comfortable certainties of the Orthodox, but somewhere in a half-glimpsed hinterland on the dirt track to Emmaus, where the Death of God meets the Resurrection, where the supernatural Christ meets the historical Jesus, and where the revolution liberates both the oppressed and the oppressors.

Welcome to Christian Alternative... a space at the edge where the light shines through.
If you have enjoyed this book, why not tell other readers by posting a review on your preferred book site.

Recent bestsellers from Christian Alternative are:

Bread Not Stones
The Autobiography of An Eventful
Life Una Kroll
The spiritual autobiography of a truly remarkable woman
and a history of the struggle for ordination in the Church of
England.
Paperback: 978-1-78279-804-0 ebook: 978-1-78279-805-7

The Quaker Way
A Rediscovery
Rex Ambler
Although fairly well known, Quakerism is not well understood.
The purpose of this book is to explain how Quakerism works as
a spiritual practice.
Paperback: 978-1-78099-657-8 ebook: 978-1-78099-658-5

Blue Sky God
The Evolution of Science and Christianity
Don MacGregor
Quantum consciousness, morphic fields and blue-sky
thinking about God and Jesus the Christ.
Paperback: 978-1-84694-937-1 ebook: 978-1-84694-938-8

Celtic Wheel of the Year
Tess Ward
An original and inspiring selection of prayers combining
Christian and Celtic Pagan traditions, and interweaving their
calendars into a single pattern of prayer for every morning and
night of the year.
Paperback: 978-1-90504-795-6

Christian Atheist
Belonging without Believing
Brian Mountford
Christian Atheists don't believe in God but miss him: especially the transcendent beauty of his music, language, ethics, and community.
Paperback: 978-1-84694-439-0 ebook: 978-1-84694-929-6

Compassion Or Apocalypse?
A Comprehensible Guide to the Thoughts of René Girard
James Warren
How René Girard changes the way we think about God and the Bible, and its relevance for our apocalypse-threatened world.
Paperback: 978-1-78279-073-0 ebook: 978-1-78279-072-3

Diary Of A Gay Priest
The Tightrope Walker
Rev. Dr. Malcolm Johnson
Full of anecdotes and amusing stories, but the Church is still a dangerous place for a gay priest.
Paperback: 978-1-78279-002-0 ebook: 978-1-78099-999-9

Do You Need God?
Exploring Different Paths to Spirituality Even For Atheists
Rory J.Q. Barnes
An unbiased guide to the building blocks of spiritual belief.
Paperback: 978-1-78279-380-9 ebook: 978-1-78279-379-3

Readers of ebooks can buy or view any of these bestsellers by clicking on the live link in the title. Most titles are published in paperback and as an ebook. Paperbacks are available in traditional bookshops. Both print and ebook formats are available online.

Find more titles and sign up to our readers' newsletter at
http://www.johnhuntpublishing.com/christianity
Follow us on Facebook at
https://www.facebook.com/ChristianAlternative